Bible Student's Study Guide

THIRTEEN LESSONS ON I, II AND III JOHN

LIFE IN THE SON

A Student Book
For Thirteen Weeks
Of Study

by
Knofel Staton

Wipf and Stock Publishers
150 West Broadway • Eugene OR 97401
2001

Thirteen Lessons on First, Second, and Third John

By Staton, Knofel
Copyright©1980 by Staton, Knofel
ISBN: 1-57910-644-7

Reprinted by *Wipf and Stock Publishers*
150 West Broadway • Eugene OR 97401

Previously published by College Press Publishing Co., 1980.

Scripture quotations are from the New American Standard Bible, © The Lockman Foundation 1960, 1962, 1963, 1968, 1971, 1972, 1973, 1975, 1977.

Dedication

This book is dedicated to two "elect ladies" who as servant-secretaries consistently practice the principles in John's epistles.

Nancy Presko   and   Marilyn Smith

Appreciation

I am greatly indebted to four people who made it possible for this manuscript to travel from my pen to the press. Nancy Presko typed the original manuscript from my terrible handwriting; Julia, my wife, edited the first copy; Marilyn Smith typed the final copy; and Don DeWelt who prompted me (more than once) to write it.

Other books by Knofel Staton:

SPIRITUAL GIFTS FOR CHRISTIANS TODAY
PARAPHRASE OF THE DECLARATION AND ADDRESS
THE GOSPEL ACCORDING TO PAUL
HOME CAN BE A HAPPY PLACE
THE PERFECT BALANCE
THE SERVANT'S CALL
YOU DON'T HAVE TO STAY THE WAY YOU ARE
THE STRUGGLE FOR FREEDOM
GROW CHRISTIAN GROW
DISCOVERING MY GIFTS FOR SERVICE
HOW TO KNOW THE WILL OF GOD
HOW TO UNDERSTAND THE BIBLE
CHECK YOUR LIFESTYLE

To be released:

MEET JESUS
CHECK YOUR CHARACTER (Beatitudes)
CHECK YOUR DISCIPLESHIP (Discipling Christians)
CHECK YOUR WAITING (Life prior to the second coming)

An Holistic and Homiletical Outline

	Page
Part One: LIFE BECAUSE OF THE SON	1
Lesson One. The Foundation and Cornerstone of the Life, 1:1-4	2

    I. The Person, v. 1
        A. His Pre-existent Reality
        B. His Earthly Reality
        C. His Post-resurrection Reality
    II. The Proclaimers, v. 2
    III. The Plan, v. 3
    IV. The Purpose, v. 4

	Page
Part Two: LIFE IN THE LIGHT	9
Lesson Two. He Lights Up Your Life, 1:5 — 2:6	10

    I. The Revelation of God, 1:5-7
        A. His Character, v. 5
        B. Our Conduct, vv. 6, 7
            1. What it is not to be, v. 6
            2. What it is to be, v. 7
    II. The Reality of Sin, v. 8
    III. The Remedy for Sin, 1:9 — 2:2
        A. On Earth, 1:9-10
        B. In Heaven, 2:1, 2
    IV. Our Responsibility with the Remedy, 2:3-6

	Page
Part Three: LIFE IN THE WALK	23
Lesson Three. The Walk of Loving, 2:7-11	24

    I. The Command of Love
        A. Its Oldness, 2:7
        B. Its Newness, 2:8a
    II. The Cause of Love, 2:8b
    III. The Contradiction, 2:9
    IV. The Continuing Power of Love, 2:10
    V. The Contrast, 2:11

	Page
Lesson Four. The Walkers Who Love, 2:12-14	32
Lesson Five. The Walk of Leaving, 2:15-29	39

    I. A Walk Away From the World's Delights, vv. 15-17
        A. The Eternal Command, v. 15
        B. The Satanic Cause, vv. 16, 17
        C. The Temporary Condition, v. 17

THIRTEEN LESSONS ON I, II AND III JOHN

      II. A Walk Away From the World's Deceiver, vv. 18-29
        A. The Chronology, v. 18
        B. The Counterfeits, v. 19
        C. The Christians, vv. 20, 21
        D. The Identifications, vv. 22, 23
        E. The Defense, vv. 24-27
        F. The Confidence, v. 28, 29

Part Four: LIFE IN THE FAMILY OF GOD 53

Lesson Six.   Chips Off the Block, 3:1-3 54
      I. A Life of Identity, 3:1
        A. The Privilege, v. 1a
        B. The Problem, v. 1b
      II. A Life of Change, 3.2, 3
        A. In the Future, v. 2
        B. In the Now, v. 3

Lesson Seven.   The Genuine Life, 3:4-10 62
      I. The Artificial Claimant, vv. 4-6
        A. He's Incompatible with Authority of God, v. 4
        B. He's Incompatible with Activity of Christ, v. 5
        C. He's Incompatible with Association with Christ, v. 6
      II. The Authentic Child, vv. 7-9
        A. He's Compatible with the Son's Behavior, vv. 7, 8
        B. He's Compatible with the Father's Begetting, v. 9
      III. An Accurate Confirmation, v. 10

Lesson Eight.   How's Your Love Life? 3:11-24 71
      I. The Commandment, v. 11
      II. The Contrast, vv. 12-15
        A. With Cain, v. 12
        B. With the World, v. 13
        C. With Death, v. 14
        D. With Hatred, v. 15
      III. The Comparison, v. 16
      IV. The Compassionate Cost, v. 17
      V. The Challenge, v. 18
      VI. The Confidence, vv. 19-24
        A. In His Position, v. 19

AN HOLISTIC AND HOMILETICAL OUTLINE

                B. With God's Persuasion, v. 20
                C. In Prayers, vv. 21-23
                D. With Christ's Presence, v. 24

Part Five: LIFE IN THE SPIRIT 83
Lesson Nine.   Professing the Divine Lord, 4:1-6 84
                I. The Call for Testing the Profession, v. 1
               II. A Criterion for Testing, vv. 2-6
                  A. The Confession of the Speakers, vv. 2, 3
                      1. When It's from the Holy Spirit, v. 2
                      2. When It's Not from the Holy Spirit, v. 3
                  B. The Character of the Hebrews, vv. 4-6
                      1. Who the Conquerors Are, v. 4
                      2. Who the Conquered Are, v. 5
                      3. What the Conflict Is, v. 6

Lesson Ten.   Practicing the Divine Life, 4:7 — 5:5 93
                I. The Cause of Love, vv. 7, 8
               II. The Character of God's Love, vv. 9, 10
              III. Our Obligation With God's Love, vv. 11, 12
                  A. The Responsibility, v. 11
                  B. The Result, v. 12
              IV. Some Certainties in Love, vv. 13-18
                  A. Our Present Consolation, vv. 13-16
                  B. Our Future Confidence, vv. 17, 18
               V. The Sharing of God's Love, v. 19
             VI. The Integrity of Love, vv. 20, 21
                  A. With Our Confession, v. 20
                  B. With His Commandments, v. 21
             VII. The Integration of Love, 5:1-5

Part Six: LIFE IN ASSURANCE 107
Lesson Eleven.   Life in Assurance, 5:6-21 108
                I. Our Assurance in the Historicity of Jesus,
                   vv. 6-10
                   A. The Historical Evidence, v. 6
                   B. The Holy Spirit's Evidence, v. 7
                   C. The Combined Evidence, vv. 8, 9
                   D. The Subjective Evidence, v. 10
               II. Our Assurance in Salvation, vv. 11-13
                   A. God's Promise for Us, vv. 11, 12
                   B. God's Publication to Us, v. 13
              III. Our Assurance in Prayer, vv. 14-17
                   A. A Condition for Prayer, v. 14
                   B. A Confidence in Prayer, v. 15
                   C. A Charge for Prayer, vv. 16, 17

THIRTEEN LESSONS ON I, II AND III JOHN

       IV. Our Assurance for Living in This World,
          vv. 18-21
          A. Our Sonship, vv. 18, 19
          B. Jesus' Sonship, v. 20
          C. Our Surveillance, v. 21

Part Seven: II JOHN AND III JOHN 123
II JOHN
Lesson Twelve.   Walking in Truth and Love 125
          I. The Community of Walkers, vv. 1, 2
          II. The Contribution to the Walkers, v. 3
          III. The Commendation of the Walkers, v. 4
          IV. The Commandments for the Walk, vv. 5, 6
          V. The Cautionary Walk, vv. 7-9
            A. Look Out for the Deceivers, v. 7
            B. Look Out for Yourselves, v. 8
            C. Look Out for the Correct Teaching, v. 9
          VI. The Constraints of the Walk, vv. 10, 11
          VII. The Continuation of the Communications,
             vv. 12-13

III JOHN
Lesson Thirteen. Practicing Hospitality 137
          I. A Respected Model — Gaius, vv. 1-8
            A. His Soul Prospers, vv. 1, 2
            B. His "Smiles" Multiply, vv. 3, 4
            C. His Services Promoted, vv. 5-8
              1. What? vv. 5, 6
              2. Why? vv. 7, 8
          II. A Revolting Model — Diotrephes, vv. 9, 10
            A. His Perverted Priority, v. 9
            B. His Perverted Practices, v. 10
          III. A Recommendation, vv. 11, 12
            A. For a Practice of God, v. 11
            B. For a Person of God, v. 12
          IV. A Resolution, vv. 13, 14

Introductory Background

Sixty years had passed since Jesus did his "earth-walk" when the apostle John wrote what we call "I John." Many of those who had been in the great crowds listening to the Master Teacher had died. Those who walked for the first time because He said, "Rise and take up your bed," those who saw the beauty of the flowers and the white, puffy clouds against the backdrop of the blue sky when He touched their blind eyes, those who saw darkness come at mid-day, and those who danced with joy because some of their loved ones had come back from the dead on that unforgettable Passover as three crosses could be seen above the horizon—most of those people were gone. And every one of the apostles who first traveled *with* Jesus all over Palestine and later traveled *for* Him all over the known world were silent in their graves—except John, a man now in his nineties.

Time marched on. Different political policies and philosophical propositions provided the ammunition for a two-barreled shotgun to be aimed at Christianity; and the gun was firing away—daily.

From the political side persecution was persistent. The government tried to force Christians into declaring that their political leader was also their "God," "Savior," and "Lord." Those who would not give a human leader equal billing with Jesus became the victims of a first century "holocaust." Christians were dipped in tar, attached to posts surrounding athletic arenas, and then burned like torches to provide the flood lights for their "wide-world of sports" events. Other Christians became the sporting event for the evening. They were dressed in skins of freshly killed animals and put into the arena to be food for starving dogs.

Watching violence in prime time is not a new form of entertainment. However, today Christians are in the living rooms watching the violence on television and enjoying it in the same way. Our entertainment is just as perverted as theirs was.

Christians were also being bombarded with a new philosophy — Gnosticism — which was playing havoc with their Christian understanding. This educational system taught that Jesus was not a person of historical fact, but of hysterical faith. That is, He was only the result of what people believed on their "insides," not what really happened in history. To the philosophers, Jesus was no more than a "winnie-the-pooh" kind of person.

The "modern" controversy about "Jesus of fact or Jesus of faith" is not modern at all. The current teaching at most universities and seminaries that challenges the "historical Jesus" is not from the scholarship of Ph.D.'s today, but of pagans two thousand years ago. It's left-over garbage, warmed-up in our new philosophical micro-wave educational ovens, and sprinkled over with an intellectual sauce to make it "taste" better.

For those Christians who would not swallow the Gnostic system of reducing Jesus to a "nobody" because He really didn't exist, the Gnostics provided another teaching about Jesus. They taught He had existed but not as a divine person. He was a mere human.

Those today who put Jesus on the same level as any other religious figure (Confucius, Mohammed, Buddha) and suggest that Christianity is on equal par with other religions are giving us some more warmed-over garbage that spoiled years ago. And they seek to overcome the stench with intellectual perfume.

Even though these teachings are erroneous, they have been effectual in keeping many non-believers away from Christianity — today, as well as when John wrote. But worse than that, these teachings have also caused many *Christians* to walk away from Jesus, just as they did when John wrote.

John wrote at a time when Christians were doubting their relationship with Jesus and thus their eternal life. And why not? On the one hand, intellectualism was *telling them* they were wrong. On the other hand, governmental policies were *treating them* as if they were wrong. They were being bombarded mentally (by the educators) and physically (by the politicians). They began to ask themselves, "Did we choose the right God? Do we really have eternal life? Does eternal life come from being intellectuals like the Gnostics?" (Gnosticism means knowledge. The whole system stressed salvation through knowledge.) John wrote to clear their thinking and resolve their doubts. He stressed several factors:

INTRODUCTORY BACKGROUND

1. Jesus was historical.
2. Full joy can be found only in Jesus.
3. The Christian life is not secured by intellectualism, but by the Christian's attitude about Jesus, sin, the world, other Christians, and the antichrists.
4. Christians are to hate sin and love the saints — just the opposite of the world-system at that time.
5. The Christian life is not seen in just how we think, but also in how we live ("the walk").
6. Knowing facts is not enough. The Christian must also live in fellowship with others ("love").
7. Education *per se* is not enough. The basis of education must be the teachings of Christ. That is why John stressed such things as: "this is the message we have heard from Him" (1:5), "His commandments" (2:3), "His Word" (2:5), "this is the promise which He Himself made to us" (2:25), "For this is the message which you have heard from the beginning" (3:11).

John considered whatever God, His Son, or His Spirit said or demonstrated to be *true* knowledge. Whenever John referred to knowing *truth,* he always connected it to Godly revelations. To say the opposite, regardless of degree or university status, is to be in error (1:6, 10; 2:4, 22; 4:20; 5:10).

In essence, John was saying in I John, "Don't be deceived. Stake your eternal life on Jesus, and live like it."

Twice John tells us why he wrote:

"And these things we write, so that our joy may be made complete" (1:4),

"These I have written to you who believe in the name of the Son of God, in order that you may know that you have eternal life" (5:13).

I John is more of a tract than a letter. It has no greeting and ending as letters do. It's more like a brochure entitled, "How I can know I'm a Christian and live like it."

Part One

LIFE BECAUSE OF THE SON

"The Foundation and Cornerstone of the Life" (1:1-4).

John anchors the life of the Christian to the "foundation and cornerstone" of Christianity. Jesus is the cornerstone and the eyewitness apostles and prophets make up the foundation (Eph. 2:20).

Both of these factors are emphasized in the first three verses of I John.

The Cornerstone = "What was from the beginning."
The Foundation of eyewitnesses = "What we have seen and heard we proclaim to you also."

Each of us should evaluate our position in Christianity, first of all, by the cornerstone and foundation.

Lesson One
(1:1-4)

THE FOUNDATION AND CORNERSTONE OF THE LIFE

John began by tackling the doubts of the readers and by emphasizing that a Christian must be related to both Jesus and fellow Christians. If a person doesn't do *that*, he is not a Christian regardless of how pious he appears to be. John moved from the Savior to the saints in the first three verses.

Here is an outline of John's introductory remarks:

> I. *The Person,* v. 1
>   A. His Pre-existent Reality.
>   B. His Earthly Reality.
>   C. His Post-resurrection Reality.
> II. *The Proclaimers,* v. 2
> III. *The Plan,* v. 3
> IV. *The Purpose,* v. 4

I. *The Person,* v. 1

What was from the beginning, what we have heard, what we have seen with our eyes, what we beheld and our hands handled, concerning the word of life (1:1).

CHAPTER 1 — I JOHN 1:1-4

A. His Pre-existent Reality

What was from the beginning.... While the world was trying to turn the Christian's eyes off of Jesus, John directed the spotlight where it belonged—on Jesus. To miss the real Jesus is to miss Christianity entirely and to miss Christianity is to miss both eternal life (v. 2) and joy (v. 4).

At first glance the reader doesn't know who it is that was from the beginning, but we don't have to read far to know that **what was from the beginning** is Jesus. Here are the obvious clues that tell us:

1. **What was from the beginning** is called the **Word of Life**. Elsewhere John indentified the Word with Jesus.

"In the beginning was the Word . . . and the Word became flesh and dwelt among us . . . and we beheld His glory, glory as of the only begotten" (John 1:1-14).

2. This **Word of Life** is referred to as **The Eternal Life** (v. 2). Later, John identified Jesus as "eternal life" (5:20).

3. John said this one was **with the Father** (v. 2). Elsewhere he spoke about Jesus being "with the Father" (John 1:1-2). Jesus also spoke about being with the Father before His earthly existence (John 17:5).

4. John spoke about being a witness to **what was from the beginning** (vv. 1-2). Later, He made it clear that the witness concerned God's Son, Jesus (5:10).

John was taking the readers back to the reality of Jesus' existence before Bethlehem. It is true that Jesus appeared in Bethlehem as a baby, but it is not true that Jesus *began* in Bethlehem. Jesus is older than that town. When time began, Jesus was there. In fact, He was the co-creator with God. "For in Him all things were created. . . ." (Col. 1:16).

What does this say to us? Among many things it says is that although Christianity is relatively new *on earth,* it is not new *in heaven.* God had planned for Christ, Christianity, and Christians from before the creation (Eph. 1:4). No one has wanted you and me as long as God has.

Christianity was not pulled out of God's hat as a rabbit is pulled out of a magician's hat. Christianity is not the result of any culture or the appearance in history of some "super star," resulting in a new religion. If we want to trace our rootage to a date, we've got to go all the way back —to the very beginning, to the creation. Christianity is not manufactured, but Godufactured. Jesus was *beyond* history. But He didn't stay *beyond* history. He came to us in our time.

B. His Earthly Reality

What we have heard, what we have seen with our eyes.

The song says it well, "Heaven came down and glory filled our souls." What was from the beginning appeared in Bethlehem. Those who claim that Jesus was just the product of people's imaginations have not studied history. He was as real as Washington, Lincoln, and you. In fact, He could be proven scientifically as can any reality. The senses agree — He was really here. He was *heard, seen,* and *touched.* That's three senses out of five. John could have added "he was smelled," but why bring the nose into it? We normally do not prove a person's existence with the nose.

John was saying, "O.K. some of you weren't around when Jesus was, but that doesn't mean *He* wasn't around." To ward off anyone claiming that John just "saw" Jesus with his imagination, he added **with our eyes.**

John used an interesting verb tense for hearing and seeing Jesus. It's a perfect tense in the Greek which stresses abiding *results.* John was testifying that he himself was the kind of person he was because he was in the presence of Jesus. How about you? Are you different? But you may answer, I've never been in the presence of Jesus. Oh? Read on. You will find that Jesus' presence lives inside of you right now — if you are a Christian.

C. His Post-resurrected Reality.

What we beheld and our hands handled concerning the word of life.

To further prove Jesus' historicity, John used the word "beheld" which meant a careful investigation, not just a passing glance. It emphasized a planned, purposeful investigation. The verb tense was changed (aorist), probably to spotlight a definite occasion when this examination took place. It took place when the disciples needed a careful look to believe that Jesus was alive after the cross (Luke 24:38-39). In fact, Jesus allowed people to see Him for forty days. No wonder His resurrection was never questioned, even by Christianity's opponents, in the first century. He had allowed too many people to see Him.

He was called the WORD because He was God's communication in flesh. See Him, and you see God. Hear Him, and you hear God. He came to make God known (John 1:18). That's why when He said, "Peace, be still," the storms retreated.

When God speaks, things happen. Power is tied to His speech. He can tell the sun to appear, and there it is. God has to be careful what He says, because what He says happens. Nature listens to Him. But the big question is — do we?

CHAPTER 1 I JOHN 1:1-4

Because He didn't remain in the grave He is called the *Word of life.* That means the Word which is life. "In Him was life" (John 1:4). That's why we live if we are united with Him. To be united with Jesus is to be united with eternal life. If you don't want to live, stay away from Jesus. He came that we might have life, and have it more abundantly (John 10:10).

II. *The Proclaimers,* v. 2

And the life was manifested, and we have seen and bear witness and proclaim to you the eternal life which was with the Father and was manifested to us (1:2).

John certified the fact that talk about Jesus was not in the realm of rumor. It was based upon eyewitness accounts. The apostles accompanied Jesus from His baptism until His ascension and witnessed the resurrection (Acts 1:22). Christianity is based upon history, not hysteria — upon fact, not fiction. If you don't like truth, go somewhere else. Jesus is the truth, and Christianity is true.

John heightened the description of Jesus every time he mentioned Him — from *the life* to *the eternal life.* He again showed that heaven and earth met in Jesus. He stressed the heaven-side when he said, **which was with the Father;** and he stressed the earth-side when he said, **and was manifested to us.** In Jesus, the Eternal One met the temporary ones. The Creator met the creatures. What a beautiful picture!

Have you ever questioned the idea that God would *really* want us in heaven? After all, aren't we really too insignificant for that? But verse two ought to settle that in our minds. For if He would come to us *here,* then surely He will permit us to come to Him *there.* Jesus came and is to be proclaimed so that unity with God would happen *now,* as is pointed out in the next verse.

III. *The Plan,* v. 3

What we have seen and heard we proclaim to you also, that you also may have fellowship with us; and indeed our fellowship is with the Father, and with His Son Jesus Christ (1:3).

Why proclaim Jesus? Just so people can get to heaven? No! That's part of it, but not all of it. John said that they proclaimed Jesus in that day so **that you also may have fellowship with us.** With whom? With *us.* That is people-to-people fellowship. The word "fellowship" really means partnership. Christians are to become fellow-partners with each other on planet earth. The word "fellowship" also means commonness. To have fellowship (*koinonia*) is to have something in common. What do Christians have in common with each other? Here is a partial listing. We share the same:

THIRTEEN LESSONS ON I, II AND III JOHN

1. Father
2. Family
3. Brothers and Sisters
4. Savior
5. Book
6. Faith
7. Lord
8. Baptism
9. Body
10. Holy Spirit
11. Promises
12. Destiny

If we are going to put up with one another in heaven *forever*, we ought to start getting along with one another *now*. If we won't do it for a short time on earth, perhaps we'll be deprived of it *forever*.

Why would John mention the human fellowship before mentioning fellowship with God? Because it is often the human fellowship that seems to break down. And if that happens the outsider will want little to do with the church. We put a big barrier in front of evangelism when we fuss and fight over paint, plumbing, the preacher, or programs. Jesus prayed for unity so the world would believe (John 17:21). Shouldn't we take His prayer seriously enough to want to be living answers to it? All of us need to say, "I can answer Jesus' prayer—and I will."

But evangelizing so that people will fellowship *with us* can be a problem. Do we really want *their* fellowship? Are we willing to let "you" be *anyone*? How about people with dark (or light) skin? How about people who can't or won't dress up for Sunday? How about men who have longer hair than we have? If we really want them, how can we show it?

Who are the most neglected people in your community when it comes to receiving an invitation from the church? Can you say it and mean it, "We proclaim Jesus to you so that *you* can have fellowship with *us*?" God's plan for sending Jesus to earth is to unite us to each other (Eph. 1:9, 10). That unity is to begin here and now.

However, we don't want people to have fellowship with us because *we* are so great; but because **our fellowship is with the Father and with His Son Jesus Christ**. It is in the church that divinity and humanity meet.

No person is ever converted to loneliness. As it was not good for the first person to be alone (Gen. 2:18), it isn't good for *any* person to be alone. Man was created for fellowship. To bypass fellowship is to bypass Christianity.

IV. *The Purpose*, v. 4

And these things we write, so that our joy may be made complete (1:4).

John's purpose for writing relates to his purpose for proclaiming Jesus and God's purpose for sending Jesus. He proclaimed Jesus so that fellowship could happen. Now he will write about maintaining that fellowship so our *joy may be complete*.

CHAPTER 1   I JOHN 1:1-4

The word "complete" is from the Greek word for "full." When fellowship is empty, joy is drained. Whatever hinders fellowship dampens our joy; whatever heightens fellowship fills up our joy. Fellowship and joy go together like a horse and carriage. You can't have one without the other.

Isn't it interesting that God's purpose for our life is our joy? Sometimes I get the impression that some Christians think it is a sin to enjoy living. Some think that laughter in the church is out of place. What a delight to know that God plans for our joy!

The world will not be very impressed by us if we are a bunch of down-in-the-mouth, complaining cry-babies. What do we need to pour into our fellowship with God and each other that will fill up our joy? If you are interested in that, read the rest of I John. That's why John wrote it — **that our joy may be made complete.** And as you read it, list the ingredients in John's recipe for joy. It won't be the same as the world's. But it works.

DISCUSSION QUESTIONS:

1. Since we today haven't had the same sense experience (see, hear, touch) as the apostles had with Jesus, can we be as sure about Him as they were? How?
2. How can we show that we want others to fellowship with us?
3. Who are the most neglected people in your community? What can you and your class do about it? When will you start?
4. List several factors in I John that will fill up our joy.
5. Why are Christians sometimes uncomfortable with joy?
6. Do we really want everyone to hear about Jesus and have fellowship with us?
   a. At what level do we want them to fellowship?
   b. How about:
      (1) boys or men with long hair?
      (2) black skinned people (or blue-eyed people — what's the difference?)
      (3) non-resident college students or military people?
      (4) people who do not dress up for Sunday?

Part Two

LIFE IN THE LIGHT

"He Lights Up Your Life" (1:5 — 2:6)

John moves from the cornerstone and foundation of Christianity (1:1-4) to the character of God (1:5).

Christians who want to check their position in Christianity need to evaluate whether or not they are united to the *real* God. We can't be united to Him without His light living in us; and when *that* happens, changes take place.

Christianity is demonstrated by morality, not just mysticism; by conduct, not just claims; by our walk, not just our talk.

Lesson Two
(1:5 — 2:6)

HE LIGHTS UP YOUR LIFE

I. The Revelation of God 1:5-7
   A. His character v. 5
   B. Our conduct vv. 6, 7
      1. What it is not to be v. 6
      2. What it is to be v. 7
II. The Reality of Sin v. 8
III. The Remedy for Sin 1:9 — 2:2
   A. On earth 1:9, 10
   B. In Heaven 2:1, 2
IV. Our Responsibility with the Remedy 2:3-6

Our joy as Christians is based upon our fellowship with God and with each other (1:3, 4). But do we know who the *real* God is? God does not change His character to fit into what we want Him to be. If anyone is to change, it must be us. We are to measure ourselves by Him, not vice versa. Consequently, we must begin by viewing both God and ourselves correctly. Only then will fellowship and joy really happen.

CHAPTER 1   I JOHN 1:5 — 2:6

I. *The Revelation of God, vv. 5-7*
   A. *His Character, v. 5*

And this is the message we have heard from Him and announce to you, that God is light and in Him there is no darkness at all (1:5).

And this is the message we have heard from Him and announce to you. John had God's communication system down pat; he was passing on what he had received from Jesus. It is because the apostles spoke Jesus' message, not their own, that the church was "built upon the foundation of the apostles, prophets, Jesus Christ being the chief cornerstone" (Eph. 2:20).

The message John heard from Jesus began with the statement, **that God is light and in Him there is no darkness at all.** "Light" in the New Testament describes a person's *mental* and *moral* state. To be "light" mentally is to have knowledge. To be "light" morally is to have purity. God is both intellectually and morally correct. And He doesn't have to *try* to be that way; He *is* that way.

John used a very strong negative to emphasize that there was no darkness in God. He was really saying, "there is *not one bit of* darkness in Him." What an amazing statement! Darkness is all around God (the Devil sees to that) but none is *in* Him.

As Christians we are recreated in God's image. If He lives in us, light lives in us as well. And light always cancels darkness. Thus, we do not have to let our surrounding culture rub off on us. We are never to be sponges soaking in the world around us (Rom. 12:1-2). Partnership with God means partnership with His character; our characters must be transformed. It is not possible to really be connected with God and not change.

After John discussed God's pure character, he moved to correcting three erroneous ideas about the Christian life. Each of these ideas begin with the phrase, **if we say,** and they appear in verses 6, 8 and 10.

   B. *Our Conduct, vv. 6-7*
      1. What it is *not* to be.

If we say that we have fellowship with Him and yet walk in the darkness, we lie and do not practice the truth (1:6).

The *first* erroneous idea about the Christian life is that Christians can live as they want to. The person who comes to Jesus singing "Just As I Am" and then goes back into the world "just as he was" may declare verbally that he *has* fellowship with God, but he would be telling a *lie.* Fellowship (*koinonia*) means partnership. One can't have partnership with "light" and walk in "darkness." That's as impossible as being submerged in a submarine and claiming to be lying on the deck in the sun.

God doesn't save us *in* our sin but *from* our sin. It is quite possible that some Christians put much emphasis on salvation but forget about maturity. Some of the Corinthian Christians seemed to think along those lines. One of the members daily lived in sin, and the church bragged about it (I Cor. 5). Paul reminded them that righteousness had no partnership with lawlessness, nor light with darkness (II Cor. 6:14).

It is one thing for sin to walk all around us (the Devil will see to that). It is another thing, however, for us to walk *in* sin. "Walk" refers to our habitual life-style (2:6). John was not saying that we *never* sin as Christians. But he was saying that sin must not be our characteristic conduct (John 8:12). The whining plea, "But I'm entitled to keep one little sin" is not Biblical. We are only entitled to become more like Christ every day (II Cor. 3:18). God has given us that ability by giving His Spirit to us. We should claim it and commit ourselves to it (Eph. 4:15).

Fellowship with Christ is to affect both what we say and what we do. We are to *do* the truth as well as say it. If we say one thing and live another, we are modeling pseudo-Christianity. So let's get on with "walking the talk," not just "talking the walk."

2. What it *is* to be.

But if we walk in the light as he himself is in the light, we have fellowship with one another, and the blood of Jesus His Son cleanses us from all sin (1:7).

John had just explained that **God is light.** Thus to be walking **in light** is to be walking **in God.** That's why John said we are to walk in light **as He Himself is in the light.** That's an order to live like God. As *He* does it, we are to do it. And why not? He lives inside of us; He has put light inside of us (Eph. 2:22).

Can we objectively know how God lives in the light? Certainly. We can look at Jesus who came to make God's way visible to us. In Jesus, God put on flesh and walked around as a personal "show and tell" (John 1:1, 14, 18). When we've seen Jesus, we've seen the Father (John 14:9).

When Jesus said, "Follow Me," He was saying, "Walk as I walk, and you will walk in the light." It becomes imperative for Christians to study closely Jesus' actions and reactions. He is not only the "show and tell" for what *God* is like, but also for how *we* are to live.

After John gave the proper model, he introduced a couple of tests to enable us to evaluate if we are living as Jesus lived. The first one deals with what *we* will be doing, while the second one deals with what *Jesus* will be doing for us.

The *first* test is whether or not we are fellowshipping with one another. How can we gauge whether or not we are walking in the light? Check our fellowship. Our fellowship with one another mirrors our walk with God. The way we treat God's children is understood by Him as being the way we treat Him. Jesus made that connection clear when He told Paul that persecuting God's people was the same as persecuting Jesus (Acts 9:4). Jesus earlier declared that whatever we do or not do to the least of God's people we do or not do to Jesus (Matt. 25:31-48). We cannot claim fellowship with God and at the same time have quarrels and maintain factions with God's people. We must all quit thinking, "God and *me*"; we must think, "God and *we*."

The move from fellowship with God (v. 6) to fellowship with one another (v. 7) was also one of Paul's major points. After speaking about fellowship with God (Eph. 2:18, 4:6, 24), he spoke about fellowship with others. But just what is involved in fellowship with one another at the practical level? It includes the following and much more: Speaking the truth, not letting the sun go down on your anger, not stealing from one another, letting bitterness be put away, being kind to one another, forgiving, loving, building up, admonishing, greeting, giving preference to the other, being devoted to the other, not gossiping, weeping with those who weep, rejoicing with those who rejoice, and serving one another.

The *second* test is what Jesus is doing for us: **The blood of Jesus His Son cleanses us from all sin.**

Blood was related to life early in Scripture (Lev. 17:11). It is the "life" of Jesus that *continues* to cleanse us from sin—not just His life on the cross that was once *shed for* us, but also His life which has been *shared in* us via His Spirit. **Cleanses** is a present tense verb which stresses an on-going cleansing. If that is not going on, we are not walking in the light.

There is a two way activity—Jesus' and ours. 1) Jesus cleanses us partly for the purpose of better enabling us to fellowship with others the way He would. He doesn't cleanse us for monastery living. He cleanses us so that *He Himself* can care for others *through us.* 2) However, if we do not maintain a proper fellowship with others *after* Jesus has cleansed us of a particular kind of selfish action or reaction, we block His further cleansing power. He Himself said, "If you do not forgive men, then your Father will not forgive your transgressions" (Matt. 6:15). We pervert His cleansing when we use it only for ourselves.

That is why the two tests—fellowship with others and the continuous cleansing of Jesus—were put together in this verse. If we are not going through a daily transformation into His likeness, perhaps we should evaluate our relationship with the rest of God's family. Are we blocking His cleansing and maturing of us because of our self-centeredness? Jesus told a classic parable about the way this two-way activity works in Matthew 18:23-35. God forgave one person a debt which was equal to 60 million days' pay! (Try to figure up how much *that* was.) But the forgiven man would not pass on that kind of cleansing to his fellowman. He wouldn't forgive his brother of a little debt which was equal to only 100 days' pay. In that lack of fellowship he blocked off God's grace.

II. *The Reality of Sin,* v. 8

If we say that we have no sin, we are deceiving ourselves, and the truth is not in us (1:8).

While the first error about the Christian life is to think that in Christ our sins make no difference (v. 6), the *second* error is just the opposite. It is to claim that we have no sin at all—we're perfect. If the devil can get us to think we are perfect, we will decide that we do not need God; thus, we will think that we have nothing to repent of or confess. If that happens, we will have deceived ourselves and miss God's forgiveness.

If we say we have no sin, the truth is not *in* us. It may be all around us, for other people will tell us we have sin. But truth is not *in* us as long as we refuse to face up to the reality of sin. No one is so void of knowledge and truth as the person who thinks he is sinless. And no one is so helpless. On the other hand, accepting the reality of sin is a step toward receiving the remedy for sin.

III. *The Remedy for Sin.* 1:9 — 2:2

   A. On earth 1:9-10

If we confess our sins, He is faithful and righteous to forgive us our sins and to cleanse us from all unrighteousness (1:9).

While the blood of Christ continues to cleanse us from all sin (v. 7), we Christians are not totally passive. We have the responsibility of fellowshipping with the saints (v. 7) and of confessing our sins. To fail to confess is equal to thinking we have no sin (v. 8). Each of us must set aside the idea that we are infallible. Only one is infallible—God.

This verse is good news for the person who thinks that when he falls *into* sin, he falls *out* of the family of God. *No,* we don't keep coming into and getting kicked out of God's family. Instead, as children we confess to our Father sins; and we do it without fear of Him.

"Confess" literally means to "speak like." When we confess our sins, our lips speak like our hearts. Inwardly, we know we have sinned; instead of covering it up and allowing it to fester (Prov. 28:13), we uncover it in the presence of God. We outwardly admit what we inwardly know. Only then can we be helped.

But confession isn't just speaking on the outside what we know on the inside. It is also to "speak like" God does about the sin. God condemns the sin, and so should we. That means our confession must be coupled with repentance. But when we confess (and repent), God forgives us; we need to "speak like" God about our sins and forgive ourselves also.

This verse does not give us the right to keep confessing the same sins over and over again. When God forgives, He forgets (Heb. 10:17); and so should we. We are not cleansed if we keep thinking about the sin. In fact, a continual re-run of the sin in our minds could keep us on such a guilt trip that we do not accept God's forgiveness. If the perfect God can forgive us, then our imperfect self should forgive also.

To confess **our sins** is to admit they are *ours* and not someone else's. We can't keep blaming sins we have chosen to commit onto our environment, parents, or the devil. If we blame others, we will want them to change, rather than changing ourselves. The devil lures us, but sin comes from our yielding to his lure (James 1:12-15).

There is bad news and good news when we have sin to confess. The bad news is that we have sinned. But the good news is that **God is faithful and righteous.** God's faithfulness often refers to His consistency in keeping His promises, as it does here. If He says He will forgive, He will. And He is **righteous**. That means our sins will not change Him, but His righteousness can change us.

At this point, the beauty of the Greek has been lost in translation; for the Greek says, "Faithful is he and just *in order that* (hina) He might forgive our sins and cleanse us from all unrighteousness." Did you catch that? One purpose for God being faithful and righteous is to help us. God maintains His character *for us.*

The word "forgive" means to send away. God sends both the sin and the punishment away, while He sends cleansing to us. There's no sin that He can't cleanse. He can cleanse **all unrighteousness.** No Christian needs to think he is locked into any sin. Name it! It can be cleansed. But not if it is being continually reinforced by repetition.

God is not just interested in forgiving us, but also in changing us. The question is — is that our desire also? Do you want to be changed? Not everyone does.

If we say that we have not sinned, we make Him a liar, and His Word is not in us (1:10).

This is the *third* error about the Christian life. This sounds very similar to verse 8, but it goes beyond that verse. **Have no sin** (v. 8) and **have not sinned** are a bit different. One deals with a position (v. 8), the other with the practice (v. 10). The first says, "I am above sin." The second says,

"I never sin period." Both deny the need of Jesus' activity. What a devastating thing to say — "Jesus, I don't need you in heaven as my advocate. I'm above that in principle (v. 8) and in practice (v. 10)." These two verses which sound so similar are a bit difficult to differentiate. Perhaps this modern parallel will help. It's possible for a professor to say, "I'm not a student." He is "above" that. But it's something else for him to say "I never study." Thus, he is saying that he is not a student in position or principle, nor is he a student in practice. Both are wrong. But arrogance often will not admit it.

To disclaim commiting sin after we've become a Christian is to show that **His Word in not in us.** That's because His Word acts as a mirror to let us see Jesus and ourselves as we are. Look at Jesus. Then look at yourself. Can you say that you act and react like Him, without exception? If you can, *you* had better spend some more time with Matthew, Mark, Luke, and John.

The more we stay away from His Word, the easier it is to say, "I'm O.K. in all I think and do."

B. In heaven.

My little children, I am writing these things to you that you may not sin. And if anyone sins, we have an advocate with the Father, Jesus Christ the righteous; and He Himself is the propitiation for our sins; and not for ours only, but also for those of the whole world (2:1-2).

John addressed the readers with a tender description of love, **my little children.** It was not a belittling put-down. He was seeing them through the eyes of the Father in heaven.

After reading about the reality of sin, some might conclude: "Now that I know I'm supposed to confess sins, I'd better sin so I can have something to confess. God must expect me to sin. I'll sin a lot so He can feel good about forgiving me. Yippee!"

No! That was not John's point. He wrote to squelch the idea that if we sin we sever our relationship with God. God does not kick us out, but we do hinder our relationship. We do grieve Him.

It is much like a father and his children.

When my children sin, they do not eliminate their kinship with me; but they do cut into the relationship somewhat. When that happens, joy is lessened. John wants our joy to be filled to the brim (1:4). And it will be, if we take the initiative to admit our sins and ask for forgiveness. That heals gaps in a human family, and it also does in the heavenly family.

John isn't writing to give us permission to sin but **that you may not sin.** He wants the fellowship to be right, and the joy to be full. But **if anyone sins** (and we do), we have a wonderful thing going for us in heaven as well as on earth.

On earth, there is a battle going on as Satan is trying to deceive us into thinking that sin doesn't matter (1:6), that we are above sin in position (1:8), or that we never sin in practice (1:10). But there is also a battle going on in heaven. Satan is always accusing us (Rev. 12:10). He stands as a continual prosecuting attorney who forgets *nothing* that we've done wrong. However, his devious tactics are counterbalanced by **the Righteous One, Jesus Christ.** Jesus is also in heaven **with the Father,** and He's there as our **advocate.**

The word "advocate" (*paracletos*) literally means "one who stands along side of." It is the same word Jesus used for the coming of Himself via the Spirit in John 14:16 (the word for advocate is also translated "helper"). Jesus stands alongside us *here* and also alongside the Father *for* us there. But before Jesus is at God's side for you *there,* He must be allowed to be at your side *here* (Gal. 3:26-27). As a paraclete, He brings God to us *here.* *There* He brings us to God. When He goes to bat for us in heaven, we have a pinch hitter who will make a home run. That is good news!

As our defense attorney, He isn't lying for us. He isn't telling the Father that we didn't do wrong or that we are mentally sick, but that we admit that we have sinned. And He has already taken our rap for us, because He was executed for us. The penalty has already been issued and executed. That fact defuses the prosecutor, Satan.

Jesus is not only our defense attorney, but is also the **propitiation for our sins** (propitiation refers to the cancellation of sin). He didn't just provide the cancellation; He also became the means for taking away our sins. He took them into His body as His own (II Cor. 5:21; I Peter 2:22-24; I John 3:16).

Jesus did this not only for us (Christians), but also **for those of the whole world.** However, people cannot be forgiven without faith, and they can't believe without hearing. No wonder John proclaimed what He heard (1:1-5). And so should we (Matt. 28:19-20, Rom. 10:13-17).

IV. *Our Responsibility with the Remedy.* 2:3-6

And by this we know that we have come to know Him, if we keep His commandments. The one who says, "I have come to know Him," and does not keep His commandments, is a liar, and the truth is not in Him; but whoever keeps His word, in Him the love of God has truly been perfected. By this we know that we are in Him: The one who says He abides in Him ought himself to walk in the same manner as He walked (2:3-6).

God expects us to get our verbal commitment and our visible conduct together. It's easy to not lift our Christianity beyond our "sayings." Evidently by the end of the first century, the Christians tended to "talk it" better than to "walk it." Notice how much John stressed what they were saying:

> If we *say* that we have fellowship with Him (1:6).
> If we *say* that we have no sin (1:8).
> If we *say* that we have not sinned (1:10).
> the one who *says,* "I have come to know Him" (2:4).
> the one who *says* he abides in Him (2:6).
> the one who *says* he is in the light (2:9).
> If someone *says,* "I love God" (4:20).

Each one of those *sayings* brags about self. Not one of them brags about God. God doesn't just *listen* to us; He also *watches* us. We may convince ourselves by talking, but we won't convince God unless the talk is accompanied by the walk.

It would be closer to the Christian spirit if we talked about God, walked the life, and let others say all those nice things about us. If they cannot say them, we probably cannot mean them.

John came down pretty hard on the nice clichés Christians were using, and each time he balanced the saying with a responsibility:

Saying	*Responsibility*
we have fellowship	walk in the light
we have no sin	take another look at yourself
we have not sinned	take another look at His Word
I know Him	keep His commandments
I abide in Him	walk as He walked
I am in the light	love your brother
I love God	love your brother

The way to measure the accuracy of what we say is by the fulfillment of the responsibility. Start there and you will be true, whether you ever say it or not. But start and end with the empty words, and you will be lying, regardless of how many times you say it or how many people you get to believe it.

After reading that Jesus was the propitiation for the sins of the *whole world,* it might be tempting for everyone in the world to claim to know the Savior. After all, most people recognize at least one god and savior. But John immediately detoured any such approach by giving us a test to evaluate our claim to know God:

And by this we know we have come to know Him.

In the Greek, the tenses of the two verbs are interesting and incisive. "By this we are now knowing (present tense) that we *have* known Him" (perfect tense). The perfect tense stresses a *past knowledge* with *present results.* John is saying we can know right now whether or not we have really known Him in the past by looking at the results in our lives. What results do we look for? We look for whether or not we **keep His commandments.** That's an objective test that is to be applied in every culture. It destroys the teaching of universalism, which says everyone is saved by his own religion if he is faithful to his gods. We have only one propitiation for our sins — Jesus Christ (v. 2). And we must know Him to have Him take our case before the Father.

Being *sincerely* wrong about the identity of the Savior doesn't result in salvation. Jesus said, "I am the way, the truth, and the life: No one comes to the Father, but through me" (John 14:6). Notice Jesus didn't say through we, but me. There is only one Savior. When He said **no one** comes to the Father without Him, how many people are left over? "No one" leaves out no one.

The person who claims to know Him without keeping His commandments **is a liar, and the truth is not in him.** To know Him is to love Him. And to love Him is to obey Him. Jesus put it this way, "If you love me, you will keep my commandments" (John 14:15). Isn't that the way interpersonal relationships operate in any circumstance? When I really know my wife, I know what delights her. And because my knowledge is balanced with love, I want to do what delights her.

The word "know" here isn't the word for theoretical knowledge (*oida*). But it refers to first-hand, experiental, personal knowledge that involves commitment to the *person,* not just to facts about the person. John was saying that mere intellectual memorization of facts is not enough. Nor is intellectualism plus emotionalism enough. If our Christian enlightenment is not matched by Christian ethics, we do not really know Jesus. We prove we know Him only by our obedience. Experiential, personal knowledge is the same as having intimate partnership (fellowship) with Him; and to fellowship *with* Him is to function *for* Him. It is to walk in the light.

The Greek words for "know" and "knowledge" are used 36 times in I John. However, we do not enhance fellowship with only knowledge. Knowledge alone will always puff us up (I Cor. 8:1) and deceive us. Knowing our position must be coupled with practice. Here is a partial list of what positions John wants us to know with the practices which are to accompany and prove the knowledge.

The Right Position	*The Right Practice*
Know Him	keep His commandments, 2:3, 4
in Him	keep His Word, 2:5
Know Him	heed this writing, 2:13, 14
He is righteous	practice righteousness, 2:29

THIRTEEN LESSONS ON I, II AND III JOHN

we shall be like Him someday	purify self now, 3:2, 3
He came to take away sin	don't sin, 3:5, 6
we've passed out of death into life	love the brethren, 3:14
He laid down His life	lay down ours for the brethren, 3:16
we are of the truth	love in deed and truth, 3:18, 19
the Spirit of God	confess Jesus, 4:2
God	listen to apostles, 4:6
God	love, 4:7
God's love for us	love others, 4:16-19
love the children	keep His commandments, 5:2
we have eternal life	believe in Jesus, 5:13
He hears us	ask, 5:14, 15

Knowledge is so important that John lists that as one of the main reasons Jesus came. "And we know that the Son of God *has come,* and has given us understanding *in order that we might know Him* who is true" (I John 5:20). However, knowledge that isn't translated into transformation of life is not knowledge of God or from God. The time is long past for Christians to quit being engaged in academics just for academics' sake. We do not attend Sunday school class, seminars, or conferences for new certificates, but for new conduct. What's on our wall will make little difference when Jesus returns. It's what's in our heart. Scholarship is not an automatic yardstick for spirituality.

One of the tragedies in ministerial education is that we have slipped into being overly concerned about degrees. A Master's degree is meaningless in Christianity unless the person himself is mastered by the Master. God accredits our colleges, our degrees, and our programs, only if the lectures lead to ethical living based upon God's Book.

We are off base to encourage education only because of the need to "know more" in the midst of a "knowledge explosion" in our culture. To understand the exegesis of Hebrew and Greek while mastering world philosophy can be meaningless unless the Person of God is known and obeyed.

We know that we are in Him (v. 5) when we **keep His Word.** And when that happens **the love of God has truly been perfected** in us. The "love of God" refers to our love for God. Our love for God has reached its intended purpose (perfected) when we keep His Word. It is keeping it, not just knowing it, that proves our love.

Few things demonstrate my devotion and love to another better than when I begin copying that other person in every minute action and reaction. I may know all about Him, but until I start letting Him so influence me that I act like Him, my knowledge is not personal and intimate.

That's why John wrote **the one who says he abides in Him ought himself to walk in the same manner as He walked** (v. 6). That's *our* "show and tell." **In the same manner** refers to exactness, imitation.

God's goal for the Christian is that we become just like Jesus:

But speaking the truth in love, we are to grow up in all aspects into Him, who is the head, even Christ" (Eph. 4:15).

But we all, with unveiled face beholding as in a mirror the glory of the Lord, are being transformed into the same image from glory to glory, just as from the Lord, the Spirit (II Cor. 3:18).

For whom He foreknew, He also predestined to become conformed to the image of His Son, that He might be the firstborn among many brethren (Rom. 8:29).

A pupil is not above his teacher; but everyone, after he has been fully trained, will be like his teacher (Luke 6:40).

But we will not walk as He walked unless we **abide in Him.** "Abide" refers to a stick-to-it-ness, not just sentimentalism. Every person should become united with Jesus with the commitment to stick with Him "for better or for worse, in riches and in poverty, in health and in sickness" and to pledge Him our faithfulness forever. Does that sound like a binding wedding ceremony? It is! The church is the bride of Christ. Some days can be pretty miserable if we just look at the raging storms. But we must not forget whom we are attached to. We are attached to One who doesn't break when the wind, rain and lightning hit. Jesus made that clear on the night He was betrayed (John 15). The storm was about to hit, so 9 times Jesus said, "Abide." Abiding in Christ was compared to a branch abiding in a vine. The branch carries in it the characteristics of the life that is inside the vine. Only then does the branch really "know" the vine. So it is with the Christian. The fruit we are to bear as that branch is Christlikeness.

We are forgiven and cleansed of sin (1:9) so that we may live like Him. He is our representative in heaven (2:1) so we will be His on earth. We owe that much to God. The word **ought** is a word which really means a debt. We are indebted to God to change (1:9 — 2:2).

The remedy for our sin needs to be matched with our responsibility (debt) to the Redeemer. We are to keep His commandments, keep His Word, and walk in the same manner as He walked. Then we *really know Him,* and we will *really fellowship.*

But what does it mean to "walk as He walked"? Much of the remainder of I John will answer that for us.

QUESTIONS FOR DISCUSSION:

1. What is the significance of the saying, "God is light"?
   a. How is He light?
   b. What are the characteristics of light?

THIRTEEN LESSONS ON I, II AND III JOHN

    c. How does light affect darkness?
    d. Should a Christian stay away from people and places of darkness?
2. Were verses 8-10 written to allow us to sin? Why were they written?
3. Do you think Christians are honest enough with God? With each other?
4. What does forgiveness mean?
    a. Can we forgive and not forget? Does God?
    b. Are you holding a grudge right now?
5. How do we make God a liar if we claim we haven't sinned?
6. What relationship do verses 1-4 which speak about Jesus have to do with verses 5-10 which speak about sin and forgiveness?
7. What attitude is expressed if we fail to admit to sin?
8. If a Christian sins, is he in a lost condition again?
9. What advantages does a Christian who sins have over a non-Christian who sins?

Part Three

LIFE IN THE WALK

"The Walk of Loving" (2:7-11)

"The Walkers Who Love" (2:12-14)

"The Walk of Leaving" (2:15-29)

Immediately after John wrote that his readers should walk in the same manner as Jesus walked, he described a bit of that walk and identified the walkers.

Christians who want to test whether or not they are walking as Jesus walked should evaluate how they love their brothers and how they loathe the lusts of the world and the lures of the world's deceivers — the antichrists.

Lesson Three
(2:7-11)

THE WALK OF LOVING

    I. The Command of Love
      A. Its Oldness, 2:7
      B. Its Newness, 2:8a
    II. The Cause of Love, 2:8b
    III. The Contradiction, 2:9
    IV. The Continuing Power of Love, 2:10
    V. The Contrast, 2:11

I. The Command of Love, 2:7, 8a

A. Its Oldness

Beloved, I am not writing a new commandment to you, but an old commandment which you have had from the beginning; the old commandment is the word which you have heard (2:7).

John had just reminded his readers that their love to God and unity with God made them indebted. That indebtedness should motivate them to walk as Jesus walked. Then John began to discuss briefly some things which walking as Jesus walked would and would not involve.

First, he reminded his readers about their privileged status by calling them — **beloved.** John reminded them that they *were* loved before they were commanded *to* love. Later he said it this way, "we love, because He first loved us" (4:19).

John constantly reminded his readers that they live their Christianity from the position of being privileged and blessed people. Christians do not walk as Jesus walked by their own gumption. We don't just grit our teeth, roll up our sleeves, and walk as Jesus walked.

Just look at some of the privileges John reminded the Christians were theirs:

>fellowship with other Christians, God, and Jesus, 1:3, 4
>they are in the light, 1:7
>cleansing of Jesus' blood, 1:7
>an advocate with God, 2:1
>propitiation for our sins, 2:2
>His Word, 2:5
>they are in Him, 2:5
>forgiven sins, 2:12
>Word of God in them, 2:14
>anointed from the Holy Spirit, 2:20
>they have His promises, 2:25
>they are born of Him, 2:29
>they have the Father's love, 3:1
>they are His children, 3:2
>they have Hope, 3:3
>His seed is in men, 3:9
>He died for men, 3:16
>God abides in men, 4:12
>they have eternal life, 5:11
>He hears men, 5:15
>they have understanding, 5:20

It is because of these privileges that we can walk as Jesus walked. However, along with the privileges we also have God's commandments. It is interesting that John had just spoken about keeping commandments (v. 4) and in this verse talked about *one* commandment. Why? Because the one commandment he brought to their attention fulfills the others he had in mind. What do we know about this one commandment? We, first of all, know that it is old: **I am not writing a new commandment to you, but an old commandment.**

There are two ways to understand "old." Something can be old if it has been around a long time (age) or something can be old if it is worn out (usage), even though it is relatively new in age.

THIRTEEN LESSONS ON I, II AND III JOHN

When John said it was an **old commandment,** he was referring to the fact that it had been around **from the beginning.** The words **have had** stressed continuous action in the *past,* emphasizing that from their first day in Christianity, they had known about this commandment — the commandment to love one another.

John the Baptist described this commandment to people when he said, "let the man who has two tunics share with him who has none, and let him who has food do likewise" (Luke 3:11). Paul explained the essence of this commandment:

> Owe nothing to anyone except to love one another: for he who loves his neighbor has fulfilled the law. For this, "You shall not commit adultery, you shall not murder, you shall not steal, you shall not covet," and if there is any other commandment, it is summed up in this saying, "You shall love your neighbor as yourself." Love does no wrong to a neighbor; love therefore is the fulfillment of the law (Rom. 13:8-10).

Paul was saying that every commandment concerning morals is fulfilled in the commandment to love. In giving us all those commandments, God was showing us how to really care for others.

This commandment to love not only goes back to the reader's experience with the *new* covenant, but it also goes back to those who first experienced the *old* covenant. To them God commanded, ". . . you shall love your neighbor as yourself . . ." (Lev. 19:18). So no matter how you look at it from the standpoint of chronology (the new covenant or the old covenant), the commandment to love is old.

B. *Its Newness*

On the other hand, I am writing a new commandment to you which is true in him and in you (2:8a).

Jesus referred to its newness in John 13:34:

> A new commandment I give to you, that you love one another, even as I have loved you, that you also love one another.

But how can it be both old and new at the same time? Easily! If I had a Model-T Ford which has never been used, it would be old in time, but not in usage. Something can be old in chronology, but new in character. This commandment is just like that. It's ancient, but not functionally antiquated. It's dated, but not dilapidated; it's old, but not out-moded; it's time-bound, but not time-worn.

This commandment is new also because of the unique nature of "love." It is the kind of love that is totally unselfish. A person with this kind of love acts for the *other* person's well-being.

It is also new because Jesus was the first one to model it in perfection. And it is new because the power to do it — the Holy Spirit — is now available to all people. It's new because it is the mark of the new age or kingdom. Regardless of how often we look at it, its freshness, its uniqueness, its model, its source, its dispensation mean that the commandment is always "new." It can never get worn out, because it is a fruit of the Spirit which is eternal in its resources (Gal. 5:22) and transcultural in its expression (5:23). We can use all of it we want. We can't love too many people, too much, or too often. It's always fresh and usable.

When John said **which is true in him and in you . . . ,** he meant that *Jesus'* use of love was fresh and true, and *our* use of it will be also. Jesus never wore out love. It was new (fresh, usable) for any day and circumstance no matter how much he used it. He never exhausted it for He was drawing from an eternal spring.

Our four-year-old just had her birthday last week. She is at the stage in her life when she says daily, "I love my family." Often she will come up to me and say, "Do you know what, Daddy?" I'll answer, "What, honey?" and she'll say, "I love you." I wonder how long it will take for that to get old to me? Never! How old does a wife get before she no longer wants to hear her husband say (and mean it by backing it up with actions), "I love you"? Death comes knocking before we get too old for that. If we keep practicing love, we will be bringing something delightfully new into people's lives. It's old and new at the same time.

II. The Cause of Love, 2:8b

Because the darkness is passing away and the true light is already shining (2:8b).

The Jews had long taught about the two ages or kingdoms. The old was the kingdom of evil and darkness characterized by hatred. The new was the Kingdom of righteousness and light characterized by love. In Jesus the new Kingdom has arrived, and in Him we are transferred out of the old and into the new (Col. 1:13). When that happens, Christians taste ". . . the powers of the age to come" (Heb. 6:5). The kind of life that will exist in heaven has arrived on earth with the coming of the new kingdom. The primary characteristic of heavenly living will be love.

As Christians we should live as citizens of the new kingdom of light with the new love and not as we used to live in the old kingdom of darkness with our old hatreds. We must always allow people to see that the newness of this love is true by the way we live. They should be able to experience our actions and reactions and conclude, "It is true, that love *is* new."

THIRTEEN LESSONS ON I, II AND III JOHN

III. The Contradiction, 2:9

The one who says he is in the light and yet hates his brother is in the darkness until now (2:9).

When it comes to love, we can't just *say* it, we must also *do* it. That's why we see a big difference between verse 9 and verse 10:

"**The one who says . . .**" (v. 9),
"**The one who loves . . .**" (v. 10).

Later John wrote, "Little children, let us not love with word or with tongue, but in deed and truth" (I John 3:18). To not back up our love-declarations with love-deeds is to not love in truth. And it is to not be **in the light.** The person who is **in the light** is not just the one who claims he is in the light, but the one who acts as if he is.

Too many times our security within Christianity has rested upon our self claims. A person can be in darkness while he says he is in the light. A person can be a citizen of hell while he says he is a citizen of heaven. One of the tests to determine whether or not we are in the light or darkness is our treatment of our brother. The one who **hates his brother is in the darkness,** regardless of his Scripture memorization, attendance records, sermons, lessons, amount of money he gives, or his eloquent prayers.

Notice that John didn't say we could hate the brother who disagrees with us. If he is a brother, we are to love him. Far too often we claim that we are to love those with whom we are united in the family of God. And that's correct. But then we equate unity with conformity and call for conformity in both faith and opinions. That's where we get off base. We must have conformity in our *position* in Christ (faith) to be brothers with one another, but not in all of our *practices* (opinions). If unity rests only upon conformity in *all* matters, we cannot have unity with anyone. And especially not with God, for His ways and His thoughts are far above ours.

We must never forget that God's family (as any human family) is made up of many different people in different stages of development; people in those different stages will possess different opinions. We have four children at home. Each is in a different stage of development. But they are united with each other in spite of their differences in opinions and practices. Their unity lies in the fact that they all share the same parents. And so it is within the Christian family — we all share God as our Father, regardless of our differences.

Not hating our brother begins by recognizing him as our brother. It then moves into taking the initiative of reconciliation — very much as Joseph did with his brothers who had despised him, betrayed him, and sold him. Not hating our brother then moves toward not neglecting him. We can "hate" a person without verbally or actively despising him. All it takes to qualify for hatred is to ignore or neglect him.

Jesus described well this level of hatred when he spoke about His second coming:

> Then they themselves also will answer, saying, 'Lord, when did we see you hungry, or thirsty, or a stranger, or naked, or sick, or in prison and did not take care of you?' Then He will answer them, saying, 'Truly I say to you, to the extent that you did not do it to one of the least of these, you did not do it to me.' And these will go away into eternal punishment, but the righteous into eternal life (Matt. 25:44-46).

That eternal punishment is called "outer darkness" (Matt. 22:13). If we remain in darkness here, we will abide in darkness there.

IV. *The Continuing Power of Love,* 2:10

The one who loves his brother abides in the light and there is no cause for stumbling in him (2:10).

In contrast to the one who *says* he is in the light (v. 9) is the one who loves someone and *shows* he is in the light. And who does he love? His brother. Notice he doesn't just love those in his own religious group. He loves **his brother.** That means any *other* child of God besides himself (I John 5:1).

It is true that the Christian is also to love his enemies (Matt. 5:43-48); however, the first step is to love his brothers. Until he can get that hurdle jumped, he is just kidding himself if he thinks he can love his enemies. Paul put it this way, "So then, while we have opportunity, let us do good to all men, and especially to those who are of the household of the faith" (Gal. 6:10).

Why "especially to those who are of the household of the faith"? For one reason — the outsiders know that we do not have the capacity to love them if we can't love the insider! That's one reason Jesus prayed, "That they may all be one; even as Thou, Father, art in Me, and I in Thee, that they also may be in Us; that the world may believe that Thou didst send Me" (John 17:21).

But just what does it mean to **love**? We can mean a lot of different things by that four-letter word in English. But the Greeks used a different word each time they had a different meaning in mind. The Greek word *eros* (love) was always a one-way love — back to self. It was the "pull my own strings" kind of love or "I love you *as long* as I am personally being benefited by it." The Greek word *philia* was the two-way contribution of friends. But *agape* is the one-way love *to* and *for* the other person's benefit. It involved: (1) seeing a need in the other person, (2) moving to meet that need, (3) not counting the cost, (4) not considering how it would benefit yourself, (5) not evaluating whether or not the person deserves to have the need met, (6) speaking and acting for the other person's total benefit. That kind of love brings continuing power to an individual's life.

The continuing action is seen in the phrase **abides in the light. Abides in** has the idea of not just embracing or enjoying, but also enduring. It carries the connotation of sticking with a situation. **To abide in the light** is to abide in Jesus. And abiding in Jesus is always related to abiding in His kind of love. Jesus connected the privilege of abiding in Him to loving the brother when he said, "abide in Me" and "love one another" on the night he was betrayed (John 15). In fact, Jesus' teaching on that night (when His apostles would face difficult days) and John's writing to Christians (who are facing difficult days) are similar. Note the comparison:

John 15	*I John 1-2*
Your joy may be full,	Our joy may be complete, 1:4
Keep the commandments (plural) v. 10	Keep the commandments (plural) 2:4
This is my commandment (singular) that you love one another, v. 12 (a *new* commandment 13:34)	A new commandment (singular) love the brother, 2:8-10
My words in you, v. 7	His word, 2:5
The world hates you, v. 19	The world hates you, 3:14
You have a helper (paraclete), v. 26	You have an advocate (paraclete), 2:1
From the beginning, v. 22	From the beginning, 2:7
Kept from stumbling, 16:1	No cause for stumbling, 2:10

No cause for stumbling is also a statement of continuance. The word for stumbling (*skandalon*) was used to describe a sharp stone sticking up from the ground which would trip someone who was walking. It came to refer to any snare that tripped a person. It eventually came to refer to the trigger on a trap that when released would capture its prey. John was saying that the person who loves does not have any snare in his life that would so trip him that he would be trapped by the devil's schemes. Neither would such a person be a living snare to others. (For a good discussion of why a person with love will not trip up another person see I Cor. 8 and Rom. 14.)

V. *The Contrast,* 2:11.

But the one who hates his brother is in the darkness and walks in the darkness, and does not know where he is going because the darkness has blinded his eyes (2:11).

CHAPTER 2   I JOHN 2:7-11

This is the opposite situation from verse 10. The one who hates (will not recognize, but will ignore, and neglect) his brother has a cause for stumbling because he **is the darkness.** That darkness has **blinded his eyes.** That's why he can't recognize his brothers — the other children of God.

He has looked at the darkness so long that he is blinded. But we don't have to stay in the dark pits; therefore, if we do become blind, it is a self-made and self-perpetuated situation. It's a shame when some groups purposely blind their members from recognizing anyone outside that group as a brother or sister in Christ. People who have become blinded in this way allow their group-traditions to take priority over the gospel-truth. Not one denominational group is mentioned in the New Testament. Therefore, God's children cannot be restricted to any one group, for no such group existed as *that* group in Jesus' day.

No man is as blind as the one who *can* see, but *won't*. He **does not know where he is going** because he doesn't know where he has been or where he is. He doesn't know that as a member of the church he is in a big family room filled with God's children — multitudes of them. He thinks he's in a tiny closet with just a few. How sad!

To walk in love is to walk as Jesus did. It is to be an accurate demonstration of "life in the Son." But who is to do it? We will look at that in the next chapter.

QUESTIONS FOR DISCUSSION:

1. Why can all commandments of God be summed up in love?
2. What are the characteristics of the love of God?
3. Which one of the characteristics have you not yet developed in your life?
4. How does keeping God's commandments show that we "know" God?
5. What does it mean to abide in Christ?
6. How do we neglect our Christian brothers?
7. Who are our Christian brothers?
8. List as many ways to love a brother as possible.

Lesson Four
(2:12-14)

THE WALKERS WHO LOVE

I am writing to you, little children, because your sins are forgiven you for His name's sake. I am writing to you, fathers, because you know Him who has been from the beginning. I am writing to you, young men, because you have overcome the evil one. I have written to you, children, because you know the Father. I have written to you, fathers, because you know Him who has been from the beginning. I have written to you, young men, because you are strong, and the word of God abides in you, and you have overcome the evil one (2:12-14).

In this section, John *first* of all identifies the spiritual position of his readers. It would be easy for the readers to think that John does not see them as being saved persons. After all, John had just described people who were blind and walked in darkness. He had also mentioned those in whom God's Word was not abiding (1:10; 2:4). "Is he talking about us?" the readers might ask at this point. And someone might answer, "Of course, he is. He said at the beginning of this letter that he proclaimed Jesus **that you also may have fellowship with us** (1:4). When he said 'may' (or might), he meant he doesn't see *us* as having fellowship with him now."

John did not want his readers to think that. He was writing to Christians, and he wanted them to know it. The world's politicians and philosophers were doing their best to try to get the Christians to doubt and deny their status with God. It is a shame when the leaders in the church also do that. So John gave his readers a word of assurance — you *are* the children of God.

By identifying his readers, John also identified who should be confessing sin (1:9), denying perfection (1:10), keeping God's commandments (2:3-4), walking as Jesus walked (2:6) and loving their brothers (2:7-11). These aspects of the Christian life-style were not to be for *just* the leaders. They were for the *entire* church.

Consequently, John identified his readers in a way that included both the newborn babes in Christ and the mature elders. If he hadn't, some might ignore the admonition in this writing by thinking that it was for that "other" group in the church. No! Housewives, high school dropouts, Ph.D's, preachers, pew-sitters, and brand-new Christians — this is for you.

There are two problems in this section which have bugged commentators for years: (1) How many categories of people are listed — two or three? (2) Why did John use a present tense verb in verses 12, 13, and a past tense verb in verse 14? Let's consider those problems briefly.

(1) *The Categories of People.* Some suggest three categories of people are meant as seen by three titles — **little children, fathers,** and **young men.** Those three would mean this:

> **Little children** — new babes in Christ
> **Fathers** — spiritually mature people
> **Young men** — spiritual adolescents in Christ

However, every other time the words "little children" are used, they refer to Christians in general, regardless of their spiritual maturity (John 13:33; Gal. 4:19; I John 2:7, 28; 3:7, 18; 4:4; 5:21). The Greek word for child (*teknon*) doesn't always mean Christian, but the Greek word for *little* child does (*teknion*). Jesus even called his apostles "little children."

John wanted his readers to see that he was including all Christians (little children) and emphasized the fact that he had *all* in mind by specifying both the mature (father) and immature (young men).

It is clear that he wanted them to see themselves as Christians by mentioning some of the benefits that only Christians have: your sins are forgiven you (v. 12), you know Him (v. 13), you have overcome the evil one (v. 13), you know the Father (v. 13), you are strong (v. 14), the Word of God abides in you (v. 14), and you have overcome the evil one (v. 14).

Notice how these benefits contrast with what John said about outsiders:

THIRTEEN LESSONS ON I, II AND III JOHN

His Readers	*Outsiders*
Forgiven sins	Claim of no sin, 1:8
Know Him, the Father	A liar who claims it, 2:4
Overcome evil one, strong	Walk in darkness, 1:6, 2:11
Word of God in them	His Word not in them, 1:10

The sins of all Christians **are forgiven you for His name's sake.** Notice the present tense — **are forgiven.** These Christians were living in a forgiven state and shouldn't forget it or doubt it. We are forgiven on account of His name. In the first century to mention doing something through a "name" meant you did it through a "person." Nearly every time you see the word "name" you can substitute the word "person." (The Greeks had no word for "person" except this word for "name.") To call on the name of Jesus is to call on *Him* — it doesn't mean to just utter His "name." To be baptized into the *name* of Jesus is to be baptized into the *person* of Jesus; to take on His *name* is to take on His *person*. In saying the Christians' sins are forgiven through His name, John was reminding his readers that they weren't forgiven apart from what Jesus did on the cross.

All Christians have also known the Father. The word *know* (v. 13) is the perfect tense which stresses abiding results. The point is that their position as Christians was rooted in their knowing the Father. But how did Christians know the Father? Only through Jesus. To know Jesus is to know the Father (John 1:18; John 14:7).

Although the benefits John listed belong to all Christians, he lined up certain situations with specific people. He said the fathers (older in the faith) **have known the one from the beginning,** and that the young men (younger in the faith) **have overcome the evil one, you are strong, the word of God abides in you.**

That particular line-up may have reflected the kinds of activities in which each of them were presently engaged. The older ones tend to reminisce about the past, but they also had to face the threats of the present. Doubts may have been rising in the face of tough persecution, so John reminded them of their rootage.

The words "you know" (13, 14) are also in the perfect tense which stresses abiding results of past actions. John wanted them to know that who they were and what they had in the spiritual realm was rooted in their progressive experiential first-hand knowledge of God. So they should not let the present circumstances rock them.

That's a good point for all senior citizens to recall. Sometimes life seems to fall apart in the sunset years. Acquaintances aren't around, but problems are. Loneliness is multiplied. Disease sets in and resources

CHAPTER 2 I JOHN 2:12-14

are drained. But senior citizens should not forget whom they have known. They have known the **one from the beginning.** This reference to the Creator who was from the beginning assures us of our security. Thus none of the tough circumstances threaten to topple Him. He will still be there at the end, and so will all those who put their trust in Him.

This One **from the beginning** is the "Alpha and the Omega" (Rev. 1:8). Those are the first and last letters in the Greek alphabet. God will have not only the first word to say about history, but also the last letter. When He finishes speaking at the end of history, there will not be one letter the opponents can add. So this **one from the beginning** will **last** to the end — and beyond it. The Father we have known is the "Lord God, who is and was and who is to come, the Almighty" (Rev. 1:8). Thus the "fathers" who *have* fought the fight and yet faced possible death from the politicians can join with Paul in saying,

> I have fought the good fight, I have finished the course, I have kept the faith; in the future there is laid up for me the crown of righteousness, which the Lord, the righteous Judge, will award to me on that day; and not only to me, but also to all who have loved His appearing (II Tim. 4:7, 8).

The **young men** were those who were certainly younger in the faith, understanding, and knowledge; however, they were the ones who were in the thick of the battle on the front lines. The devil was hurling his flak at them constantly, and some may have thought about throwing in the towel. But as someone has observed, "When the going gets tough, the tough get going." John reminded them that they had been tough and still were.

These younger Christians were second-generation Christians. The torch has been passed to them as in a spiritual relay race. The fathers had passed it on to them. Now they must run with it. And John reminded them that they could.

You have overcome the evil one. Why talk about that? Because the younger ones had strong desires (II Tim. 2:22) that Satan would use to detour them from righteousness. That's Satan's approach for newer Christians. He hammers away at bringing our desires unto sinfulness. When the new Christians are also "younger ones" in age — teenagers and young adults, it is super-tough. There is so much in our culture today that pressures this age group to become conformed to the world.

But there is for the Christian the power to overcome:

> You are from God, little children and have overcome them; because greater is He who is in you than he who is in the world (4:4).

Jesus Himself has overcome the world (John 16:33), and He lives in the Christian. We are to overcome evil with good (Rom. 12:21), and we overcome by our faith (I John 5:4, 5).

In Revelation, John listed some of the rewards for overcoming the evil one:

> the tree of life in the paradise of God - Rev. 2:7
> not hurt by the second death - Rev. 2:11
> hidden manna (eternal resources) - Rev. 2:17
> white stone (victor's reward) - Rev. 2:17
> name not erased from book of life - Rev. 3:5
> Jesus acknowledges them - Rev. 3:5
> a pillar in temple of God - Rev. 3:12
> sit with Jesus on the throne - Rev. 3:21
> inherit all blessings - Rev. 21:7

When John reminded them that they **have overcome,** he reminded them not only that it was possible, but also that they had *already* experienced it in the past and were living in the victory of it in the present. Every Christian knows the experience of being stronger than Satan. It's great. It *is* possible for the Christian to overcome Satan. It is possible because God will never allow us to be tempted beyond what we are able and will with the temptation provide a way of escape (I Cor. 10:13); it is possible because we have living in us the power of the age to come (Heb. 6:5); it is possible because the one who lives in us in greater than the one who lives in the world (I John 4:4); it *is* possible because our trust is in Jesus (John 16:33).

John continued the thought by saying, **you are strong.** They overcame in the past because they were strong. However, they weren't strong simply in their own strength. John brought that out by saying, **the word of God abides in you.** That Word is both Jesus (John 1:1) and His commandments (I John 2:5, John 5:38, 10:35).

To put God's Word in us deters us from sin. The psalmist put it like this, "Thy word I have treasured in my heart, that I may not sin against Thee" (Psalm 119:11). Paul spoke about the victorious armor of the Word when he wrote, "and take . . . the sword of the Spirit, which is the word of God" (Eph. 6:17).

Overcoming is a must, but it isn't automatic. That's why John wrote about the responsibility Christians must take in avoiding a love of the world and following after persuasive deceivers (vv. 15-23) in the next section.

(2) *The Verb Tenses.* Although dealing with this problem will not affect the meaning and application of these verses, we will briefly consider it. It is more of an academic exercise than one that will alter lives.

CHAPTER 2   I JOHN 2:12-14

It is true that John used the present tense "I am writing" in verses 12-13 and the past tense "I wrote" in verse 14. The question is why? Here are some possible explanations:
- a. "I write" refers to what he was presently writing. "I wrote" refers to what he had just finished writing—1:1—2:11. The point is that both what was written in the past and what was being written in this communication is for all Christians—regardless of their level of maturity.
- b. "I write" and "I wrote" referred to the same thing, but from two different perspectives. "I wrote" from the perspective of the reader who would later read what he "wrote." This particular past tense (aorist) is used that way (epistolary usage).
- c. "I write" referred both to what he was presently writing and would write from that verse to the end of this communication. "I wrote" referred to 1:1—2:13.
- d. "I write" referred to this whole communication. "I wrote" referred to a previous writing he had already sent them—possibly the Gospel of John.

Anyone of those could be the reason. We cannot say with certainty. (However, if what he wrote [past tense] refers to the Gospel of John, then the Gospel was written to Christians to encourage them—not to non-Christians to evangelize them. Thus our common understanding of John 20:31 needs to be re-evaluated. John may not have written his Gospel so people would *start* believing that Jesus was the Messiah, but so they would *continue* believing it.)

John used the tense like this later on which may mean (b) is the best explanation.

Regardless of how we understand (or don't understand) the reason John shifted verb tenses, the reason for this section is clear. He wanted his readers to not doubt their Christian stance, but rather to delight in it. However, their delight should not desensitize them to the danger that faced them. They not only were to live in *Him*, but also in the *world*. The dangers were there for both the immature and mature Christians. Those who walk as Jesus walked (v. 6) must stay awake lest they fall. In that walk they must not only know what to live, but also what not to love. We will look at that next.

QUESTIONS FOR DISCUSSION:

1. How does the fact that the Christian's past sins were forgiven relate to loving his brother?

THIRTEEN LESSONS ON I, II AND III JOHN

2. How can you relate the condition of forgiven sins in verse 12 with the other conditions in verses 13, 14?
3. Relate the four characteristics in 2:13, 14 to each other—(1) know Him, (2) strong, (3) Word of God abides in you, (4) overcome the evil one.
4. Why did John keep reaffirming the fact that he was writing to Christians?

Lesson Five
(2:15-29)

The Walk of Leaving

I. A Walk Away From the World's Delights, 15-17
   A. The Eternal Command, v. 15
   B. The Satanic Cause, vv. 16, 17
   C. The Temporary Condition, v. 17
II. A Walk Away From the World's Deceiver, 18-29
   A. The Chronology, v. 18
   B. The Counterfeits, v. 19
   C. The Christians, vv. 20, 21
   D. The Identifications, vv. 22, 23
   E. The Defense, vv. 24-27
   F. The Confidence, vv. 28, 29

Although John wanted his readers to have assurance about their standing with God, he did not want them to be overly confident. Christians are not only to delight in their position but are also to be dedicated in their practice of the faith. Christians are commanded to "stand firm in the faith" (I Cor. 16:13). We are to put on the armor of God (Eph. 6:10), not just live in the assurance of grace. It is possible to be too settled in our security. Paul wrote the Corinthians, "Therefore let him who thinks he stands take heed lest he fall" (I Cor. 10:12). Paul made it a point in his life to buffet his body and make it a slave "lest he himself should be disqualified" (I Cor. 9:27).

So immediately after sharing with his readers a word of assurance about their "spiritual health," John wrote to them about the Satanic hazards they must avoid. John had just shared what they should love (2:7-11); then he showed what they should loathe. There are both things to love and things to loathe in the Christian walk. We get our lives messed up when we love what we should loathe and loathe what we should love.

John moved from how Christians should love their brothers to how they should not love the world-system. Paul did the same thing in Ephesians 4 and 5. Notice the parallel:

Ephesians	*I John*
as beloved Children, 5:1	little children, 2:12
walk in love, 5:2	love the brothers, 2:10
do not let immorality, or any impurity or greed even be named among you, 5:2	do not love the world, 2:15

Loving the world would erase our love to the brothers, because it would involve living for self and not for them. A walk *toward* God's children must be accompanied by a walk *away* from the Devil's charms.

I. A Walk Away From the World's Delights, 15-17

  A. *The Eternal Command,* v. 15

Do not love the world, nor the things in the world. If any one loves the world, the love of the Father is not in him (2:15).

It is possible to love too much, so God's command through John is, **Do not love the world.** At first, that sounds sensible. But then we remember that "God so loved the world" (John 3:16). If God loves the world and we are to imitate Him, why are we told *not* to love the world?

The word "world" in the Bible refers to several different things. First, it can refer to just the *physical universe* God created (John 1:10). Secondly, it can refer to the *human inhabitants* in this physical universe (John 3:16). Thirdly, it can refer to the kingdom of Satan (I John 4:4; 5:19; John 12:31; 14:30; 16:11; II Cor. 4:4; Eph. 2:2). Paul referred to this anti-godly system as "the world forces of this darkness . . . the spiritual forces of wickedness" (Eph. 6:12).

The latter meaning is primarily what we are not to love. God is certainly not suggesting that we should adopt a monastic attitude and isolate ourselves from the physical universe or from the humans in it. In fact, Jesus' entry into this world demonstrated just the opposite. He put on human

CHAPTER 2   I JOHN 2:15-29

flesh and was very much involved in the daily lives of people. He was
not an isolationist from the world, but He did keep away from the "world
forces of darkness."

To not love the **things of the world** *primarily* refers to the "delights"
that Satan dangles in front of us. Some of those "delights" are listed in
the works of the flesh: "immorality, impurity, sensuality, idolatry, sorcery,
enmities, strife, jealousy, outbursts of anger, disputes, dissensions,
factions, envyings, drunkenness, carousing, and *things* like these" (Gal.
5:19-21).

While the primary meaning is Satan's way in the world, there is a
secondary sense in which we are not to love this physical world. For
when we do, we begin to idolize it and live for the accumulation of the
things of the present world. When that happens, we do not share the things
(goods) of the world with others. Jesus told two classic parables against
such an attachment to the physical world (the Rich Fool - Luke 12:13-21
and the Rich Man and Lazarus - Luke 16:19-31) and He topped off His
teaching with an exhortation to share (Matt. 25:31-46). Hell will be the
destination for the hoarders.

God is not asking us to abhor riches. If so, we would have to abhor
God who owns everything. Some Christians have used these teachings to
prove that they *have* to live in poverty. However, this teaching does
correct a growing fad being spread by some Christian communicators —
that God wants everybody rich. Many Christians today look to wealth
as a goal to achieve on earth. We are to love what material things can
do for others (Eph. 4:28; I Tim. 6:19-19), without loving the things themselves.

These two understandings of **Love not the world nor the things of the
world** are interrelated. Because one will always lead us to the other if
we do not repent. If we start by loving the Devil's rule, he will lead us
to a devotion of this *temporary world*. If we start by loving the temporary
things in the world, we will accept the Devil's schemes — whether or
not we acknowledge that the schemes we use are his.

Either way, we shift masters. That's why John said, **If anyone loves
the world, the love of the Father is not in him.** We can't have it both ways.
That doesn't mean that God doesn't love us; it means that we don't love
Him. We can't worship both the Creator and the creation. Paul described
some people who tried it and messed up their lives:

> For they exchanged the truth of God for a lie, and worshiped and
> served the creature rather than the Creator, who is blessed forever.
> Amen (Rom. 1:25).

Jesus expressed the thought this way:

> For where your treasure is, there will your heart be also (Matt. 6:21).

No one can serve two masters; for either he will hate the one and love the other, or he will hold to one and despise the other. You cannot serve God and Mammon (Matt. 6:24).

One practical way to show our love to God is by sharing the world's goods to meet the other person's needs (Matt. 25:31-46). When we refuse to do that (and we will refuse if we love the world more than the people in the world), we refuse to love God. That is why James said, "whoever wishes to be a friend of the world makes himself an enemy of God (James 4:4). A "friend of the world" is a person who uses the things of the world primarily for his own benefit (James 4:2, 3). Later John put the thought this way:

> But whoever has the world's goods, and beholds his brother in need and closes his heart against him, how does the love of God abide in him? (I John 3:17).

Judas Iscariot was an example of loving the world's goods:

> But Judas Iscariot, one of His disciples, who was intending to betray Him, said, "Why was this ointment not sold for three hundred denarii, and given to poor people?" Now he said this, not because he was concerned about the poor, but because he was a thief, and as he had the money box, he used to pilfer what was put into it. Jesus therefore said, "Let her alone, in order that she may keep it for the day of My burial" (John 12:4-7).

Demas is also an example: "For Demas having loved this present world, has deserted me and gone to Thessalonica . . . (II Tim. 4:10). There is an interesting twist in this verse and in II Timothy. The Greek word for "love," *agape,* normally refers to an unselfish love, but here it is a selfish love. It is a reaching out to the world to benefit it for the wrong motive — for what return the world will give back to the person. It is *agape*-love that is perverted. It is the *agape*-love for darkness that Jesus spoke about (John 3:19, Matt. 5:46).

B. *The Satanic Cause,* v. 16

For all that is in the world, the lust of the flesh and the lust of the eyes and the boastful pride of life, is not from the Father, but is from the world (2:16).

This verse gives the reason we are not to love the kingdom of Satan (world). The verse begins with a Greek word that literally means "because" *(hoti).* All that is a part of the world forces of darkness is from Satan's kingdom, not from the Father's. God is love (4:16), but the world force of darkness hates us (3:13). To love the world is to love self-destruction.

CHAPTER 2   I JOHN 2:15-29

John listed three avenues through which the evilness of the world captures us: (1) the lust of the flesh, (2) the lust of the eyes, (3) the pride of life. Notice carefully that John does *not* put down the flesh, eyes, or life, but only when they are coupled with lust and pride. Lust and pride are not from the Father but from the world. John was certainly not suggesting that the materials in the world are evil. After all, God created the physical world as well as the spiritual. And John had a very high view of the created world (John 1:3, 10). Even Jesus put on physical flesh, eyes, and life (John 1:14; Phil. 2:5-7).

The word "lust" is really the word for desire. Desires can be neutral, good, or evil. Our basic desires are God-given (hunger, thirst, sex, rest, security, etc.). It is only when we seek to express them beyond the limit drawn by God that they become "lusts." This happens when Satan lures and entices us to prostitute our God-given appetites in Satan-given activities.

Blessed is a man who perseveres under trial; for once he has been approved, he will receive the crown of life, which the Lord has promised to those who love Him. Let no one say when he is tempted, "I am being tempted by God"; for God cannot be tempted by evil, and He Himself does not tempt any one. But each one is tempted when he is carried away and enticed by his own lust. Then when lust has conceived, it gives birth to sin; and when sin is accomplished, it brings forth death (James 1:12-15).

The word for "**life**" (*bios*) stresses goods, possessions, or resources. It's when we allow the possessions to puff us up that we detour ourselves from loving God. The physical (flesh), sight (eyes), or goods (life) can be used by Satan to blind us and capture our minds. When our minds are captured *by* the world *to* the world, then our manners and priorities are also captured. That's what it means to be caught in the snares of the devil (I Tim. 6:9; II Tim. 2:26). Peter described it well:

These are springs without water, and mists driven by a storm, for whom the black darkness has been reserved. For speaking out arrogant words of vanity they entice by fleshly desires, by sensuality, those who barely escape from the ones who live in error, promising them freedom while they themselves are slaves of corruption; for by what a man is overcome, by this he is enslaved. For if after they have escaped defilements of the world by the knowledge of the Lord and Savior Jesus Christ, they are again entangled in them and are overcome, the last state has become worse for them than the first. For it would be better for them not to have known the way of righteousness than having known it, to turn away from the holy commandment delivered to them. It has happened to them according to the true proverb, "A dog returns to its own vomit," and, "A sow, after washing, returns to wallowing in the mire" (II Peter 2:17-22).

C. *The Temporary Condition,* v. 17

The world is passing away, and also its lusts; but the one who does the will of God abides forever (2:17).

The temporary is able to bring only temporary satisfaction. It doesn't last. It's deceptive. It's a dandelion-kind of splendor.

This is really a second cause for not loving the world. It compares the temporary nature of the world — it **is passing away,** over against the eternal nature of the Christian — who **abides forever.** The Christian abides forever only as he abides in Christ (v. 6), who is Himself eternal (I John 5:20). To abide in Christ is to walk as Jesus walked, which is another way of describing the one **who does the will of God.**

Jesus	*The Christian*
His life	Walk the way He walks, I John 2:6
"For I have come down from heaven not to do my own will but the will of Him who sent me," (John 6:38)	Do the will of God, 2:17
Eternal One	Abides forever, 2:17

To give up abiding *forever* for the temporary life is a bad trade, but that is what we do if we live for the world (v. 16) instead of for God. This is not a scare-tactic. It is the reality of life, "for the one who sows to his own flesh shall from the flesh reap corruption, but the one who sows to the Spirit shall from the Spirit reap eternal life" (Gal. 6:8).

Although the world looks as if it is here to stay, it isn't. It is already passing away. This applies to both the physical world which is in a continual state of running down and to the spiritual world of darkness — the old kingdom which is giving way to the new kingdom. We are now living in the overlapping of the ages. The end of the old age (kingdom of darkness) is upon us and the beginning of the new (kingdom of light) already has arrived with the coming of Jesus. Jesus has ushered in the last period of time before earthly history comes to a halt. But this last stage is not a time to sleep (Rom. 13:11). Dangers are escalating during this period.

II. A Walk Away From the World's Deceiver, 18-29.

A. *The Chronology,* v. 18

Children, it is the last hour; and just as you heard that antichrist is coming, even now many antichrists have arisen; from this we know that it is the last hour (2:18).

CHAPTER 2   I JOHN 2:15-29

John spotlighted the urgency of alertness by telescoping the last "age" into the last "hour." This doesn't mean the last sixty minutes of existence. Literally, the Greek doesn't say "the" last hour but "a" last hour. It does mean that we are in the last sequence of time before the Second Coming. This last sequence is elsewhere referred to as the last time (I Peter 1:5, 20; Jude 19), latter times (I Tim. 4:1), last days (Acts 2:17; Heb. 1:2; James 5:3), and the hour (Rom. 13:11). This "last hour" covers the entire span of time from Jesus' first coming to His Second Coming. Christians were warned that antichrists would come (Matt. 24:5, 24), and they are still among us.

Throughout this entire span of time, Christians will have to face the dangers of the antichrist — not just one, but **many antichrists.** The word antichrist literally means "against the Messiah." An antichrist is not against the *idea* of a messiah, but against the *identity* of the messiah being Jesus. This is the first time the word "antichrist" appears in the Bible. Only John used the term, but the concept appears in many places (2:18, 22; 4:3; II John 7).

To say they **have come** (perfect tense) is to stress the negative abiding results from them. But how can we know **that it is the last hour** because **many antichrists have arisen?** Antichrists would not have come if the Christ had not come. The fact we have antichrists adds evidence to the fact that the authentic Christ has preceded them. Since the coming of Christ ushered in the new Kingdom (last age, later days, last times, last hour), we know that *that* is already upon us.

But who are the antichrists? They often come disguised as imposters or counterfeits of real Christians.

B. *The Counterfeits,* v. 19

They went out from us, but they were not really of us; for if they had been of us, they would have remained with us; but they went out, in order that it might be shown that they all are not of us (2:19).

A counterfeit is an imitation of the real thing. It's difficult to tell a good counterfeit from the real thing. The most effective antichrist is the best counterfeit. The biggest danger to Christianity does not come from "atheistic" antichrists but from those who by all appearance are a part of the church. A few Christians are always led astray (like sheep) more quickly when false doctrine comes from within the fold than from without. After all, we trust those from within to be speaking the Word of God in a manner pleasing to God.

Always be alert; for the devil loves to disguise himself as an angel of light (II Cor. 11:14), and it isn't beneath him to use the persuasive speech of a sincere preacher, evangelist, T.V. performer, elder, deacon, professor of religion, Sunday school teacher, radio preacher, etc. Don't let a person's role fool you. We must test the spirits (I John 4:1).

Paul wrote that such a thing would happen within the eldership at Ephesus:

> I know that after my departure savage wolves will come in among you, not sparing the flock; and from among your own selves men will arise, speaking perverse things, to draw away the disciples after them (Acts 20:29-30).

John evidently had a certain group of antichrists in mind who at one time were a part of Christanity, for he said: **They went out from us.** Some suggest that they never were Christians because John said, **But they were not of us.** But the Greek does not support the idea. The Greek for **from us** and **of us** is the same (ex *hemon*). The answer to what this means lies in the verb tense of **were** which is the imperfect tense. This tense can stress a continuation in the past. It seems likely that John was saying they did not *continue* with the body of Christians. Indeed they went out from (they *had* been a part of us) but did not continue with them. Consequently, they did not represent the position of the Christians, although some may think they did.

The antichrists' present beliefs and teachings proved that they didn't have continual oneness with the Christian community. Outer appearance isn't enough to judge the sincerity of Christians. Eventually, the counterfeits will be shown up — **in order that it might be shown that they all are not of us.** Paul taught the same thing in I Corinthians 11:19:

> For there must also be factions among you, in order that those who are approved may have become evident among you.

If the counterfeits aren't spotted and identified during this life, they will be at the end of this age. Although not all people on the earth may be able to tell who is and who is not the Lord's, God knows His own (I Tim. 2:19) and will not be fooled when He returns.

C. *The Christians,* vv. 20, 21

But you have an anointing from the Holy One, and you all know. I have not written to you because you do not know the truth, but because you do know it, and because no lie is of the truth (2:20, 21).

John did again what he had done earlier in verses 11 and 12. He reassured his readers that he didn't have them in mind when he spoke about some who were not still a part of the fellowship. He contrasted the outsider of verse 19 with his readers; they *were not continuing,* **but you have** (continuous state) **an anointing from the Holy One.** The anointing is the Holy Spirit (II Cor. 1:21; Eph. 1:13; I John 2:27) which Jesus who is the Holy One (Mark 1:24; John 6:69; Acts 2:27; 3:14) has sent (Acts 2:33).

To be anointed with the Holy Spirit is to put on Christ (Gal. 3:20, 27).

CHAPTER 2   I JOHN 2:15-29

Thus the word for Christ (*Christos*) and the word for anointing (*chrisma*) are similar. The *ma* ending stresses result. The action of anointing (*chrisma*) is the result of the divine anointed one — Christ (*Christos*).

John affirmed that his readers knew something, **and you all know.** What is it they know? In this context, they knew that the antichrists are denying that Jesus is the Messiah (v. 22). They just don't know "truth," they know the truth. Usually when the definite article is placed in front of the word "truth" in the New Testament, it is in reference to Jesus (John 3:21; 5:33; 8:32, 40, 44, 45; 14:6, 17; 15:26; 16:7, 13; 17:17; 18:37; Rom. 1:18, 25; 2:8, 20; 3:7; I Cor. 13:6; II Cor. 4:2; 13:8; Gal. 2:5, 14; Eph. 1:13; 4:24; Col. 1:5; II Thess. 2:10, 12; I Tim. 3:15; 4:3; 6:5; II Tim. 2:15, 18; 3:8; 4:4; Titus 1:14; Heb. 10:26; James 1:18, 5:19; I Peter 1:22; II Peter 2:2; I John 1:6; 2:4; 21; 3:19; 4:6; 5:6; II John 1, 2; III John 3, 4, 8, 12).

Since Jesus does not lie, He is not the source of any lie that comes from people who claim to be His. The ultimate source of all lies is the Devil (John 8:44). Thus the antichrists are the devil's apostles whether they knew it or not. But the big lie in this context was that Jesus was an imposter.

D. *The Identifications*, vv. 22, 23

Who is the liar but the one who denies that Jesus is the Christ? This is the antichrist, the one who denies the Father and the Son. Whoever denies the Son does not have the Father; the one who confesses the Son has the Father also (2:22, 23).

Throughout the centuries people have put people's names on the antichrists. John wasn't thinking about names (although I am sure he could have named some). Instead John described the antichrists generally; so that when the specific people he might have had in mind died, this writing would not cease to be relevant. Antichrists were not restricted to the first century. They will live throughout this entire final chapter in earthly history.

Christians in certain groups often call anyone not in their religious group the antichrists. But John did not do that. He didn't tag the label of "antichrist" onto those who held different opinions. The "antichrist" refers to just one kind of person — the person who **denies that Jesus is the Christ. This is the antichrist, the one who denies the Father and the Son.**

It is extremely dangerous to tag the label of antichrist on anyone else. We must understand that Christians will differ in opinions about many things because we are at different levels of maturity in the family of God. That should not surprise us. We should expect it when we understand how any family works. To claim that anyone who differs from us isn't accepting the inspiration of the Scriptures or the deity of Jesus and thus is an antichrist is mere sectarianism. It comes close to claiming that *our* understanding of the Scriptures is infallible.

The antichrist is the one who denies the Son. It's as simple as that. A person can be in error about many doctrines without being an antichrist. But he can't be in error about the deity of Jesus without being an antichrist.

A person's relationship to God is directly related to his acceptance or denial of Jesus, for to deny Jesus is to deny the primary way we know God (Heb. 1:2; John 8:19; 14:6; 16:13; 17:3). So to deny Jesus is to oppose the doctrine of God.

Whoever denies the Son does not have the Father; the one who confesses the Son has the Father also (2:23).

A person has only two courses to take — confession or condemnation. Confession may be *temporarily* costly as it may invite persecution. However, condemnation is *eternally* costly. It results in being cut off from the fellowship (v. 19), being called a liar (v. 22), and being without God (v. 23). It's not possible to believe in God and not Jesus. The final result will be Hell. But to confess (speak like the Father and the facts) is to be united to the Father and to have a grand future. In the first century, those who confessed the deity of Jesus were immersed into Him, became clothed with Him in the act of faith (Gal. 3:26, 27), and were promised eternal life (I John 2:25).

Notice that John said the Christian must confess two things: (1) His sin (1:9) and (2) God's Son as the Messiah. These two are essentially related. If we don't confess sin, we have no need for the Son. If we don't confess the Son, we have no remedy for our problems. To confess Jesus is to acknowledge God's provision for that problem. To deny either is to be lost.

The deniers will cringe at the Second Coming of Jesus, but the confessors will have confidence (3:28). However, confidence at His Second Coming is not an automatic guarantee for everyone who can confess the Lordship of Jesus with their lips:

> Not everyone who says to Me, "Lord, Lord," will enter the kingdom of heaven; but he who does the will of My Father, who is in heaven. Many will say to Me on that day, "Lord, Lord, did we not prophesy in Your name, and in Your name cast out demons, and in Your name perform many miracles?" And then I will declare to them, "I never knew you; depart from Me, you who practice lawlessness"
>
> (Matt. 7:21-23).

The "lip" confession must be coupled with the "life" commitment. That's what abiding in the Son is all about.

E. *The Defense,* vv. 24-27

As for you, let that abide in you which you heard from the beginning. If what you heard from the beginning abides in you, you

CHAPTER 2   I JOHN 2:15-29

> also will abide in the Son and in the Father. And this is the promise which He Himself made to us: eternal life. These things I have written to you concerning those who are trying to deceive you. And as for you, the anointing which you received from Him abides in you, and you have no need for any one to teach you; but as His anointing teaches you about all things, and is true and is not a lie, and just as it has taught you, you abide in Him (2:24-27).

John began with the phrase **as for you** in order to contrast his readers with the antichrist. While the antichrists were abandoning what they had heard about Jesus, John's readers were to abide in what they had heard **from the beginning.** That is their primary defense against becoming deceived (v. 26).

But what had they heard from the beginning? In the context of I John, they heard what we read in 1:1-3. (Notice the phrase **from the beginning** in both 1:1 and 2:24.) **From the beginning** they had heard that Jesus was **the Word of life** (1:1), the eternal life who was with the Father (1:2), and His Son and the Christ (1:3). In addition to that, He is the advocate, the righteous one, and the cancellation of our sins (2:1-2).

The best way to stick with those doctrines about Jesus is to refuse to listen to any arguments or lectures given by people who deny the deity of Jesus. In the name of religion, many seminaries have watered down the deity of Jesus as a result of humanistic philosophy. A Christian should refuse to attend or support such an institution, regardless of its prestige in the educational circle. No school is eduationally sound that denies the Emmanuel. Paul wrote to Timothy to pay no attention to speculative teaching which can shipwreck the faith of Christians (I Tim. 1:3-4, 19).

The reward of heaven is only for those who let the Christian message about Jesus remain in them (v. 25). Jesus made the promise conditional and will conditionally carry it out (John 3:15; 4:14, 6:40; 17:3). If we allow the truth about Jesus to find a home in our hearts now, we will find a home in His heaven later.

But we must be on guard because the antichrists are out to deceive the Christians (v. 26). Their main tactic is to lure lambs away from the flock by their magnetic teaching. If it were not possible for them to do it, John would not have spent so much time warning his readers against them.

Christians do not have to be led astray, for they have the indwelling Holy Spirit, **As for you, the anointing which you received from Him abides in you.** That Holy Spirit is the source of all Christian teaching. But how has the Holy Spirit taught them about all things? First of all, through the apostles whom the Holy Spirit inspired (John 14-16). But secondly, through the written Word which the Holy Spirit also inspired. Christians are to abide in the truth inspired by the Holy Spirit.

THIRTEEN LESSONS ON I, II AND III JOHN

What did John mean when he said, **and you have no need for anyone to teach you?** Certainly he didn't mean that humans could not teach Christians, for John himself was instructing Christians. Christians are clearly to teach fellow Christians:

> Go therefore and make disciples of all the nations, baptizing them in the name of the Father and the Son and the Holy Spirit, teaching them to observe all that I have commanded you; and lo, I am with you always, even to the end of the age (Matt. 28:19-20).

> Let the word of Christ richly dwell within you; with all wisdom teaching and admonishing one another with psalms and hymns and spiritual songs, singing with thankfulness in your hearts to God (Col. 3:16).

> Prescribe and teach these things (I Tim. 4:11).

> And the things which you have heard from me in the presence of many witnesses, these entrust to faithful men, who will be able to teach others also (II Tim. 2:2).

> For though by this time you ought to be teachers, you have need again for some one to teach you the elementary principles of the oracles of God, and you have come to need milk and not solid food (Heb. 5:12).

It is clear by these other passages that John was not condemning Christians teaching Christians. But in this context, John did not want his readers to listen to the teachings of the antichrists. The emphasis was not that the Christians should not have human teachers, but that they shouldn't listen to just *anyone*. Just because a person claims to be a teacher with something to say doesn't mean we have to listen. Evidently, John realized that those antichrists who were at one time a part of the fellowship became deceived by listening to false teachers. So John told his readers to not follow suit.

We are to abide in Christ, and in order to do that His Words must abide in us (John 15:7, 10). The person who will not accept Jesus as the divine messenger certainly would not communicate Jesus as divine. The Christian is to be teachable but not just by anyone and everyone. We have a responsibility to test the teachers (4:1). The primary test of a proper teacher is the teacher's acknowledgment of Jesus as the Messiah from God (4:2-3). If he doesn't then forget about his teaching. He is an antichrist who would like to deceive you. There is too much at stake to play games.

F. *The Confidence,* vv. 28-29

And now, little children, abide in Him, so that if He should appear, we may have confidence and not shrink away from Him in shame

at His coming. If you know that He is righteous, you know that every one also who practices righteousness is born of Him (2:28-29).

While the antichrists did not abide in Him as seen by the fact that they did not remain in the fellowship (v. 19) and did not remain with the faith (v. 22), those in the faith must remain in Christ in order to have confidence at Jesus' Second Coming.

John didn't say "if" Jesus appears, but **when** (although the Greek words are the same). That Jesus is coming back is certain, but when He is to come is not. This is the great "uncertain certainty" in the Bible. Even Jesus didn't know when (Matt. 24:36). His return will be like a thief who doesn't send us his calendar ahead of time (Matt. 24:43). It will be at the time we do not expect (Matt. 24:44). So when you think you've got it all figured out—forget it. If Jesus didn't get it figured out, you won't.

What's our responsibility then? Be ready! That's it. When Jesus taught about His Second Coming He repeated two truths—(1) No one will know when, (2) but everyone must be ready (Matt. 24:36, 39, 42, 44, 46, 50; 25:13).

If we abide in Him, we will have **confidence** when He returns. Some Christians are suspicious about being confident as if there is something wrong in it. We can be confident in what we trust. Do we trust God, His promises, and Jesus' ability to save? If so, then confidence should mark us now and then.

Confidence at Jesus' Second Coming will be expressed by the person who does **not shrink away from Him.** But many will shrink away:

> And the kings of the earth and the great men and the commanders and the rich and the strong and every slave and free man, hid themselves in the caves and among the rocks of the mountains; and they said to the mountains and to the rocks, "Fall on us and hide us from the presence of Him who sits on the throne, and from the wrath of the Lamb; for the great day of their wrath has come; and who is able to stand?" (Rev. 6:15-17).

At one time I thought *all* people (even Christians) should run and hide when Jesus returns. How wrong I was. The Christian who has been abiding will not run *from* Him but *to* Him with thanksgiving and praises. The antichrists will shrink away, but the Christians will scramble toward Him. What will make the difference? Our abiding in Him before He returns.

We can have confidence at His coming because we know we are in His family,

If you know that He is righteous, you know that every one also who practices righteousness is born of Him (2:29).

THIRTEEN LESSONS ON I, II AND III JOHN

To practice righteousness doesn't mean to be perfect. Remember "if we say we have no sin we deceive ourselves" (1:8). The one **who practices righteousness** is the one who has been making righteousness his dominant life-style. He may have flaws and setbacks, but righteousness is still the *characteristic way* he lives.

The word righteousness has two important aspects to it. It refers to being declared righteous (being *acquitted*) and being *equipped* to live righteously. The acquittal comes from our *pardoned relationship* with God—He forgave us. Our *equipping* comes from our *paternal relationship* with God—He fathered us. In Christ we were **born of Him.** He put His equipment (life, seed, Spirit) in us. From that time on, we daily mature more and more into His likeness. Each of us will be somewhere in that progress of maturity when Jesus returns *if* we are abiding with Him. Anyone who is progressing in maturity is practicing righteousness, regardless of where he is on that line of maturity. Are you progressing in maturity or determined to stay the way you are? Some will be spiritual babes, adolescents, teenagers, and the more mature. The confidence of the growing babe will be just as solid as the confidence of the more mature ones at the Second Coming.

It will be like a family reunion. When I come home from a trip *all* my children run to greet me—from the four-year-old to the teenager. They don't evaluate who is and who is not the most mature. They don't immediately think about all the wrongs they've done while I was away.

So it is with God's family reunion when Jesus returns. Those who have not stuck with Christ will run away. Those who have will run toward Him. How about you? Which will it be? Are you abiding? Does your life now demonstrate that you are **born of Him?** Are you abiding? If so, you will be progressing from bearing fruit to bearing *more* fruit, and from bearing *more* fruit to bearing *much* fruit. That's the natural result of abiding (John 15:2, 5). That's the life-style of the children of God. But to do it, we must walk as Jesus walked (I John 2:6), by taking the walk of love (2:7-11) and, at the same time, walking away from the world's delights (2:15-17) and from the world's deceiver (2:18-23). To walk away from that now is to run toward Jesus later.

QUESTIONS FOR DISCUSSION:

1. Discuss how to relate John 3:16 with I John 2:15?
2. What is lust of the flesh in your life?
3. What is lust of the eyes in your life?
4. What is pride of life in your life?
5. When is the last hour?
6. When are we anointed?
7. What is the relationship of the Holy Spirit to truth?
8. How does a person deny that Jesus is the Christ? List specific ways.
9. What are the evidences that a person is abiding in Christ?

Part Four

LIFE IN THE FAMILY OF GOD

"Chips Off the Block" 3:1-3
"The Genuine Life" 3:4-10
"How's Your Love Life?" 3:11-24

After John introduced the idea that the Christian is born of God (2:29), he discussed what it meant to live in the family of God (3:1-24). It involves not only what we *are* as children (3:1-2) but what we can become (3:2-3). However, the Christian life isn't just looking ahead to what we will become. It also involves a present life-style of morality, love, confidence, and obedience.

Lesson Six
(3:1-3)

"Chips Off the Block"

  I. A Life of Identity, 3:1
    A. The Privilege, v. 1a
    B. The Problem, v. 1b
 II. A Life of Change, 3:2-3
    A. In the Future, v. 2
    B. In the Now, v. 3

John had just introduced the idea that Christians are born of God (2:29). So it was only natural for him to pick up the idea of life in the family of God.

I. A Life of Identity, v. 1

See how great a love the Father has bestowed upon us, that we should be called children of God; and such we are. For this reason the world does not know us, because it did not know Him (3:1).

  A. The Privilege, v. 1a

It would be possible for a reader to race right past the phrase "born of Him" (2:29), so John planted a "stop sign" in the word **see.** It's the

54

CHAPTER 3   I JOHN 3:1-3

word for "behold" (*idou*). The idea is "slow down, reader, look and listen. I've got something for you to look at closely."

What is it John wanted us to see? He wanted us to see what God gave us — **How great a love the Father has bestowed upon us.** The English translation loses the excitement of the Greek word **how great** (*potapos*). *Potapos* is an adjective that stresses breath-taking amazement, astonishment, admiration, and excitement. It literally means "of what country." The idea is that whatever is being described is so fantastic that it is completely foreign to our experiences. It is "out of this world." When the winds obeyed Jesus, people asked, "What kind (*potapos*) of a man is this, that even the winds and the sea obey Him?" (Matt. 8:27). To say merely "kind" is too weak. They were saying, "What an astonishing, fantastic, amazing person this is. He's so great that we have nothing compared to Him in our culture. He's foreign to us." It was the same word Mary used to describe the angel's greetings to her — "what kind of salutation," fantastically marvellous (Luke 1:29). Peter used the word to describe the kind of people we are to be as we wait for the Second Coming of Jesus (II Pet. 3:11). We are to be a *potapos* people — fantastically, amazingly, astonishing people. In fact, our life-style should be foreign to that of the earth.

It is so easy to overlook the little word "that," but it is a most significant word. It stresses *purpose* (*hina*). God has given us this breath-taking love for a *purpose that* **we should be called children of God.** He wants to be identified with us and wants us to be identified with Him. He likes to introduce us as His children. Think about the beauty of that thought.

We have several children who live in our area. Sometimes I'll have a bunch of them mixed in among some of my own children at the park or some other activity. On occasion someone will say, "It's nice to see your children." And I'll quickly reply, "Oh, they (and I'll point out the ones I mean) aren't my children." There are some children I do not want *anyone* thinking that they are mine. (In fact, there *are* times when I do not even want people thinking mine are mine. Have you ever had those moments — like the time a whole section of cereal boxes comes tumbling down at the supermarket?) It would take an "out of this world" kind of love for me to introduce *some* children as mine, but God is not embarrassed to do that for us. He has given to us His love for the purpose of introducing us as His — with all our hang-ups, dumbness, stupidity, slowness, and arrogance. He says, "Meet my child." What love!

I heard about a woman who hired a researcher to trace her family tree and write a biography of her life. To her amazement, she discovered that one of her grandfathers, whom she had not known, had died in the electric chair at Sing Sing. She asked the biographer if he could report that fact in a way so as to not embarrass her, and here's what he wrote: "Her grandfather occupied the chair of electricity in one of America's most noted institutions. He was very much attached to his position and literally died in the harness." What a classic example of embarrassment.

However, God *wants* to claim kinship with us. But notice — just because He has given His love doesn't mean we are automatically His children. He gave it so that we **should be** or *might be* called His children. Whatever He gives (bestows) must be received by us to benefit us.

But who wants to just be **called** someone's child? It's much better to *really* be that person's child. John dealt with that reality. He made clear that God didn't give us His love just so He could use some empty meaningless words. He calls us His children because we are — **as such we are.** This isn't fiction: it's fact! His calling us His children is not a "snow job"; it's sincere. How? Because in Jesus Christ we were *born of God* (2:28 — 3:9). We receive the gift of childhood in God's family by receiving Jesus (Jn. 1:12); and we receive Jesus by putting Him on through faith, repentance, and immersion (Gal. 3:26-28).

In Jesus Christ, God accomplished His most astonishing miracle. He both adopts us (Eph. 1:5; Rom. 8:15) and begets us. No human can do both of those. Only God can. To be adopted by God would have been great enough. In the first century, an adoption changed the status of the child. His name was changed; his family was changed; debts were cancelled; and he automatically became a citizen of the country of his parents. In a similar way, all of that becomes ours when God adopts us. What privileges! What more could we receive?

One thing more — God's seed (*sperma*) living us. And *that* precise miracle takes place along with adoption (I John 3:9; 2:28; John 3:3-8). No wonder John used an exciting, fantastic, "out of this world" word to describe this love. Nothing on earth can be compared to it. It would be marvellous to be known (and to be) as God's friend, or God's neighbor, or God's paper boy, or God's barber — but God's *child*!! John had lived with that truth for sixty years and couldn't describe it in human terms. However, being God's child isn't all "peaches and cream."

B. The Problem, v. 1b

For this reason the world does not know us, because it did not know Him (3:1b).

We should be delighted (not disturbed) when the world does not know us with a personal, experiential, understanding kind of knowledge (*ginosko*). When the world is giving us flak, it's natural to ask whether God is on our side or is punishing us. Some of John's readers were asking that very question in the face of their tough times. So John defused that line of thinking by saying that troubles were happening because they

CHAPTER 3 I JOHN 3:1-3

were God's, not because they were *not*. On the night Jesus was betrayed, He said to His apostles, "if the world hates you, you know that it has hated me before it hated you" (John 15:18). For emphasis Jesus repeated the statement twice (John 15:21, 16:3). Why should the world have a love affair with us when it didn't with Jesus (John 1:10)?

The world hating God, Jesus, and the church is like a drowning man trying to beat off the lifeguard who has come to save him. Christians exist to serve all mankind. That's the living sacrifice we offer. The drowning world will often strike out at us, but we aren't to let the world take us down into the murky waters with it. As children of God, we are to allow the life-style gap between us and the world to get wider and wider as we progress toward becoming more like Jesus.

II. A Life of Change, 3:2-3
   A. In the Future, v. 2

Beloved, now we are children of God, and it has not appeared as yet what we shall be. We know that, when He appears, we shall be like Him, because we shall see Him just as He is (3:2).

For emphasis, John repeated two of the significant teachings that were discussed in verse one: Christians have been loved (*beloved*) and as a result are **children of God.** Those two realities are *present* realities — NOW. We don't have to wait for them.

However, there is a waiting period in the lives of all children as they slowly become what they shall be. Children love to look ahead to what they might become and dream about it. Our four-year-old is daily declaring, "I want to grow up." When we ask her why, she always has something in mind she wants to become — a nurse, a mother, a student.

As children of God we are becomers, for each Christian is an unfinished product. There is the "now" and the "not yet" aspect in each of us. We are "now" children of God, but we are "not yet" what we shall become. Here are some letters each Christian could have etched on a plaque somewhere in his house, office, or place of business — H P W M F G I N F W M Y. When people ask about the meaning of such "nonsense" letters, he can reply: "**H**ave **p**atience **w**ith **m**e **f**or **G**od **i**s **n**ot **f**inished **w**ith **m**e **y**et."

At first, John sounds as if he is contradicting himself when he said on the one hand **it has not appeared yet what we shall be**; and then on the other hand, he said **we shall be like Him.** But that's no contradiction at all. It's another one of those uncertain certainties in the Bible. It is *certain* that we shall be like Him, but it is *uncertain* all that will be involved! There is so much more that will be included in OUR FUTURE:

Things which eye has not seen and ear has not heard, and which have not entered the heart of man, all that God has prepared for those who love Him (I Cor 2:9).

THIRTEEN LESSONS ON I, II AND III JOHN

When Jesus walked on the earth, only a glimpse of His majesty could be seen. He emptied Himself before He came (Phil. 2:5). **We know that, when He appears, we shall be like Him.** The word **appear** means "make manifest." How could it possibly be made manifest or clear to us what we will be like, if we haven't fully seen what He is like? When He comes back it will all be clear, **because we shall see Him just as He is** — not as He became for His earth-walk, but as He is in His totality. And it won't be as if we're looking into a mirror (His reflection on the pages of the Bible). We shall see Him face to face (Matt. 5:8; John 17:24; I Cor. 13:12; II Cor. 5:7; Heb. 12:14; I Pet. 1:8; Rev. 1:7; 22:4).

Becoming like Him doesn't mean that we will lose our unique personalities, but that we will immerse our personalities into His character. Each person is so unique that there are no two sets of fingerprints or vocal cords alike. We are valuable partly because we are rare. But each person is also pliable. We take on some of the characteristics of people around us while keeping our own individual uniqueness. So it will be with the Christian when Jesus returns. We shall be like Him while our uniqueness will remain.

The sequence is important. First, He shall appear. Secondly, we shall see Him. Thirdly, we shall be like Him. But that sequence doesn't mean that we just sit around twiddling our thumbs waiting for that transformation to take place. Oh no! Heaven is a prepared place for a prepared people. Transformation into His likeness *begins* now and *finishes* then. God will not finish then what we are not beginning now.

B. *In the Now,* v. 3

And everyone who has this hope fixed on him purifies himself, just as He is pure (3:3).

The person who wants to become like Jesus *then* does something about it *now*. That's the transforming power of hope. Hope always looks ahead to a goal. Psychologists are now telling us that man's present behavior is more strongly determined by his goal orientations and motivations to reach out for them than by his past experiences. Gordon Allport says that in order to be "normal" a person needs to have a defining objective — a "line of promise," a "directedness," or "intentionality." Hope is needed as well as love and faith for Christian development and expression. And all three of these are included as part of the family life in this one chapter. (Hope, v. 3; love, vv. 1, 2, 11, 14, 16, 17, 18, 23; and faith, v. 23).

A real hope is always an acting hope. It gets things done. That's why it is called a "living hope" (I Pet. 1:3). And that real hope is based on a certain amount of evidence. It is more than an inner feeling or superstition. For instance, if I were to call my wife and say, "Honey, prepare dinner for five more people; I have a 'feeling' we are going to have company." That kind of "hope" wouldn't cause Julia to prepare an extra potato. But if I said, "Honey, I just got a call from the Smiths: they are fifty miles away and planning to stop by. We'll be having five more for dinner." Hope based on evidence will cause Julia to prepare. A girl who has a wedding date set (with a boy in mind) will *do* something about that hope. She'll send out invitations, prepare her ceremony, plan her wardrobe, and wash her hair the night before. Real hope always acts. It motivates us to get things done.

Do you really hope to become like Jesus when He appears? Whether you do or not is tested by what that hope is motivating you to do here and now. God will not be impressed by our "thrill" of being like Him later, if we aren't just as thrilled in becoming like Him now.

Children love to study their heroes, imitate them, be in their presence, buy products they endorse, etc. So it should be with the disciples of Jesus. If we want to be just as He is later, we will be studying what we can know about Him now and be changing into His character (II Cor. 3:18). We are to be in the process of partial and continual transformation (Rom. 12:1) if we expect to experience the product of completed transformation.

But what can we know about Jesus before He comes back? We can know what He was like during His earth visit. And John summed that up into one word — PURE.

The word "pure" (*hagnos*) stresses the idea of being dedicated to the service of God. It involves separating yourself from anything that would hinder you from doing or being what God intended you to do or be. Are sin and selfishness blocking your usefulness to God and others? Is anything interfering with your living in the family of God with the life-style of the Father? Purity doesn't refer to a white-wash job — appearing to be pure on the outside. It refers to the inside being as pure as the outside. It's the opposite of hypocrisy (Matt. 23:25, 26). The "pure in heart" shall see God as He is (Matt. 5:8).

So if you want to be like Jesus later, you must be daily becoming **just as He is** now. The words **just as** (*kathos*) stress exact correspondence. The words are used in many different ways. Here's a partial listing (1) Jesus had exact correspondence (*kathos*) with God (John 5:30; 6:57; 8:28; 12:50; 14:31). (2) The New Testament events exactly correspond with the Old Testament predictions (Mark 1:2; Matt. 26:24; John 6:31; 7:38; 12:14; Rom. 1:17; 4:17; 8:36; 9:13; Heb. 3:7; 4:3). (3) Christians are to have exact correspondence with:

>Apostolic teaching - Col. 1:26-27; 2:7
>Apostolic character - Phil. 2:17
>Jesus' walk - I John 2:6

THIRTEEN LESSONS ON I, II AND III JOHN

Jesus' purity - I John 3:2-3
Jesus' righteousness - I John 3:7
Jesus' love - I John 3:23, John 13:34
Jesus' life-style - I John 4:17
God's mercy - Luke 6:36
Jesus' conduct - John 13:15, 34; 15:12
Unity as Jesus and the Father have - John 17:11, 21
God's forgiveness - Eph. 4:32; Col. 3:13
Love of wife just as God loves church - Eph. 5:25

We can use this as an evaluation check list. How's your exact correspondence doing? It's easy to say, "But I can't." That's not true. The issue is not "I can't," but "I won't." We *can* because these areas are the family life-style, and we have been born into the family with God's seed given to us (I John 3:9).

If we do not want to become like Him here, we will not become like Him there. We need to check our *desire*. Do you *desire* to be like Him? As children we will imitate someone. God wants us to desire to be a "chip off His block."

When I was a small lad, I saw a poem in a dimestore I bought for my Father. It's still in a frame, but now it's hanging in our son's room. At the top of the poem is a picture of a father dog and his pup which looks identical to the father. The words from an anonymous author are these:

> When folks tell me I'm like you, Dad,
> I almost burst with pride
> Cause ever since I was a pup
> A-standing by your side,
> I've liked the way you faced the world,
> The things you say and do
> And would be glad to be the chip
> Off such a block — as YOU!

The greatest tribute we can give to another is to want to be like that person.

Wouldn't it be great if that poem would express our admiration of God and our desire to be like Him by being like His Son Jesus, who was the exact image of God?

If that's not our desire here, it won't be our delight there. Let's change into His likeness — today — and every day!

QUESTIONS FOR DISCUSSION:

1. What is the connection between 3:1 and 2:29?
2. Why does being called a child of God reveal God's great love?

CHAPTER 3   I JOHN 3:1-3

3. How does the second coming motivate us to purity now?
4. How does the world show it hates us?
5. What specific reactions should we have toward the world's hatred?
6. In what ways will we change after Christ returns?
7. In what ways should we now change?

Lesson Seven
(3:4-10)

The Genuine Life

I. The Artificial Claimant, vv. 4-6
   A. He's Incompatible with Authority of God, v. 4
   B. He's Incompatible with Activity of Christ, v. 5
   C. He's Incompatible with Association with Christ, v. 6
II. The Authentic Child, vv. 7-9
   A. He's Compatible with the Son's Behavior, vv. 7, 8
   B. He's Compatible with the Father's Begetting, v. 9
III. An Accurate Confirmation, v. 10

Anyone can "claim" to be a child of God, and he can "prove" it with the evidence of having been baptized and having membership in the church. But self-claims aren't equal to genuineness. In the rest of this chapter, John discussed three tests by which the fakes could be unmasked. (1) What's his moral life like? (vv. 4-10) (2) What's his love life like? (vv. 11-22) (3) What's his belief like? (vv. 23-24).

This wasn't the first time John had discussed these "tests," and it would not be the last time. By utilizing these tests, the Christian can erase doubt about his position with God; and at the same time, the counterfeits can be revealed. Here's a list of these tests applied at different places:

CHAPTER 3 I JOHN 3:4-10

The Belief Test	The Moral Test	The Love Test
(His attitude about Jesus)	(His attitude about sin and righteousness)	(His attitude about his brother)
3:23	1:5 — 2:6	2:7-11
4:1, 2	2:12	3:11-22
4:16	2:13b	4:7-12
5:1	2:14b	4:16-21
5:4	2:15-17	5:2
5:10	2:29 — 3:10	
5:13	5:3-4	
	5:16-19	

These three tests unmask the artificial child of God and contrast him with the authentic child of God. If we have any doubts about the legitimacy of a person's position with God as he flips his doctrine in front of us, we can apply these tests to him. The teaching of every cult will fail one or more of these tests. Don't be dazzled by the sensational. And don't be lured by the "logical" approach to religion that some propose. The devil is logical and sensational, but he cannot pass these tests. To fail even one of these tests is to be an artificial Christian.

I. The Artificial Claimant, vv. 4-6

   A. He's Incompatible with Authority of God, v. 4

Every one who practices sin also practices lawlessness; and sin is lawlessness (3:4).

Sin matters! But the Gnostic philosophers had popularized the idea that sin didn't affect a person's spirituality at all. Their reasoning went like this: Anything phsyical is evil; since the body is physical, it is evil; so sin in and through the body is natural. However, the spirit inside man is good and cannot be touched or affected by evil done by the body. It is just the body that sins, not the spirit. Consequently, sin is just "skin" deep. Its affect doesn't penetrate and pollute the spirit. So go ahead and sin!

No wonder that philosophy caught on fast. It's like saying that the "X" rated is as acceptable as the "G" rated. It really doesn't matter.

In direct contradiction to that teaching, John wrote that sin *does* matter. Here are some of his teachings about the person who sins or claims to be without sin:

               Doesn't have fellowship with God - 1:5
               Deceiving the self (the *whole* self) - 1:8
               Makes God a liar - 1:10
               The truth is not in that person - 1:8

God's Word is not in that person - 1:10
Doesn't know God - 2:4
Not forgiven - 2:12
Hasn't overcome the evil one - 2:13
Is not strong - 2:14
Loves the world system - 2:15-17
Doesn't have hope - 3:3
Is without law - 3:4
Doesn't abide in Christ - 3:6
Doesn't know Christ - 3:6
Is of the devil - 3:8
Is a child of the devil - 3:10
Doesn't love God - 5:3
Isn't born of God - 5:4
Doesn't have faith - 5:4
Is unrighteous - 5:17
Is in the power of the evil one - 5:19

Any one of those conditions is serious; but ADD all of them up, and the end result is devastating. John dramatically opposed any teaching that whitewashed the seriousness of sin.

John didn't allow a person's social status, benevolent deeds, religious knowledge, or anything else to get the sinner off the hook. He called it as it was when he said, ANYONE. Five times in this section he said ANYONE. There are no double standards in Christianity. It makes no difference who the person is, if he **practices sin he also practices lawlessness; and sin is lawlessness.**

John did not define sin with some kind of philosophical, environmental, or cultural cover-up job. His definition was both simple and profound — **sin is lawlessness.** The word **lawlessness** (*anomia*) literally means without law. But John was not talking about just *any* kind of law. A person could be following every law of his religious group or of his country and still be practicing **lawlessness.** To be without law in this context means that a person is not keeping God's commandments (3:22), is not loving the brother (3:11), and is not believing in Jesus (3:23). It means that a person is living his life without God. *To live without law is to live as if there is no God.*

But anyone who will not honor *the* One Creator-God will select some other "god" and live by the law of *that* substitute "god." Some people make up their own law and obey self rather than God. The first temptation the devil hurled at man was the lure for man to become his own "god" — "you will be like God . . ." (Gen. 3:5). The mark of arrogance is no better displayed than when a person becomes his own "god." That's the epitome of selfishness. That kind of philosophy for living will always result in hurting other people. It's not by accident that John moved from the activity of lawlessness to the activity of hatred (v. 15).

Some Christians today get uneasy about the idea of *any* law in Christianity. It is true that in Christ we have been freed from *the* Law (Old Testament covenant), but we are not freed from law *per se*. With the liberty we have in Christ comes law. In fact, we read about the "law of liberty" (James 1:25—2:12) which is the "royal law" (James 2:8), or "the law of Christ" (Gal. 6:2). God's "law" in the new covenant is the commandments of Christ. They are the boundaries God has set for living with each other in the midst of an immoral environment. Without these boundaries, we would go into our own ways as children will do when all external restraint and guidelines are removed. God did not give us new birth to usher us into total permissiveness. Before the end of the first century, some Christians thought that Christianity equaled no law. But John corrected that idea — **sin is lawlessness.**

Was John saying that anyone who sins *once* is in a state of lawlessness? No! He was talking about the person who persistently sins as an habitual pattern of his life. That's why he used the present tense verb **practices** (*poieo*) which literally means, "continues doing." The person who makes sin a part of his life-style contradicts the authority of God, and is not an authentic child of God. Remember, the child of God is in the process of purifying himself (v. 3).

If a persuasive speaker with dynamite "charisma" comes to town, take a look at his moral life. If it's characterized by pollution, he is not speaking as a servant of God, regardless of what book or phrases he uses. Had those of the People's Temple understood this, they might have abandoned Jim Jones. John exposed all the Jim Joneses who have or will ever exist.

B. He's Incompatible with the Activity of Christ, v. 5

And you know that He appeared in order to take away sins; and in Him there is no sin (3:5).

The person who fails the moral test is at odds with the work of Christ, for Christ came to **take away sins.** The words **take away** also mean to take up or lift. Jesus lifted sins off of us and took them into Himself on the cross (I Pet. 2:24; Heb. 9:28; II Cor. 5:21). He both took sins *up* and took them *away.* He took them *up* to the cross, and He took them away to the grave. And in that act He tasted the condemnation that sin earned for us (Heb. 9:5); He became our substitute. That's why there is no condemnation for those whose lives are united with Him (Rom. 8:1).

If the best example of a child of God — Jesus — came to take away sins, then all of God's other authentic children should live to keep sin away. Whoever doesn't do so is restoring what Jesus came to remove. The authentic Christian does not live in contradiction to the *work* of Christ. Nor does the authentic Christian live in contradiction to the *character* of Christ. John spotlighted Jesus' character when he said, **and in Him there is no sin.**

The church is called the bride of Christ. That means we are to be faithful to Him. However, the artificial bride has little interest in that. The church is also called the body of Christ. An artificial body has no interest in the work and character of its head. However, an authentic body is supremely interested in maintaining both coordination and cooperation with the work and character of its head. But to do that calls for committed associations, which is what the fake runs from.

C. He's Incompatible with Association with Christ, v. 6

No one who abides in Him sins; no one who sins has seen Him or knows Him (3:6).

Many things in life do not mix. Instead they stand so opposite to one another that they repudiate each other. For instance, light and darkness do not mix. God and the devil do not mix. Oil and water do not mix. By the same token, a continuous committed abiding in Christ does not mix with sin when it is the ruling principle in one's life. A person who keeps letting sin be his life-style demonstrates that he is an artificial child of God. Such a life-style proves that he hasn't really seen or known the real Jesus. To "see" refers to understanding Jesus. To "know" Him refers to being united with Jesus. Understanding Jesus and unity with Jesus result in a transformation of life that continues. That's the resulting power of abiding (John 15). As a person cannot abide in air without breathing it, so a person cannot abide in Christ without living as He lived.

But don't we have a contradiction in John's teaching here? Doesn't this verse violate 1:8? Look at them side by side:

1:8	3:6
If we say we have no sin we deceive ourselves . . .	No one who abides in Him sins . . .

On the one hand, it sounds as if John is saying that if we say we do *not* sin we are lying. But on the other hand, if we say we are Christians and *do* sin, we are lying. Has he got us all in a trap? No! Not at all! There is no contradiction. In 1:8, he was talking about perfection. In 3:6 he was talking about persistence. Christians are *not perfect;* that's why we need Jesus as our advocate with the Father (2:1); but at the same time, Christians are *not persistently sinning* either. We are all at different stages of growth. In those stages, we will fall at times (Gal. 6:1). Paul wrote to churches that had sin problems. He wrote to help mature them. However, it is quite another thing if sin is the ruling principle of our lives.

The artificial Christian's life-style lives in contradiction to the authority of God, the activity of Christ, and association with Christ. But the authentic Christian lives in harmony with all of that.

II. The Authentic Child, vv. 7-9

  A. He's Compatible with the Son's Behavior, vv. 7, 8

Little children, let no one deceive you; the one who practices righteousness is righteous, just as He is righteous; the one who practices sin is of the devil; for the devil has sinned from the beginning. The Son of God appeared for this purpose, that He destroy the works of the devil (3:7, 8).

People are so eaily led astray. But no one should be deceived about who is a Christian (**little children**) and who is not a Christian (**is of the devil**). Christians can be known by their fruit.

Beware of the false prophets, who come to you in sheep's clothing, but inwardly are ravenous wolves. You will know them by their fruits. Grapes are not gathered from thorn bushes, nor figs from thistles, are they? Even so every good tree bears good fruit; but the rotten tree bears bad fruit, nor can a rotten tree produce good fruit. Every tree that does not bear good fruit is cut down and thrown into the fire. So then, you will know them by their fruits. Not every one who says to Me, 'Lord, Lord,' will enter the kingdom of heaven; but he who does the will of My Father, who is in heaven. Many will say to Me on that day, 'Lord, Lord, did we not prophesy in Your name, and in Your name cast out demons, and in Your name perform many miracles?' And then I will declare to them, 'I never knew you; depart from Me, you who practice lawlessness' (Matt. 7:15-23).

We must not only hear God's law; we must practice it (Matt. 7:24-27). As "the proof is in the pudding" when talking of food, the "proof is in the practice" when speaking of Christianity. The authentic Christian's life-style (practices — present tense) is aligned with Jesus' life-style — **just as He is righteous.** To be righteous involves three things, (1) to be *acquitted* of sin — justified, forgiven, (2) to be *equipped* with God's seed (v. 9), (3) to be *committed* to live it.

Those of Satan and those of the Savior live in contradiction to each other because the devil and Jesus live in contradiction to each other (v. 8). The devil **has sinned from the beginning.** Literally, the Greek says that the devil is sinning (present tense) **from the beginning.** The point is that he started sinning at the beginning and is still doing it. Sin is the ruling principle in his life. How far back does **from the beginning** go in this context? It could refer to one of the following: (1) from the beginning of sin. The devil started it and is keeping it alive. (2) From the beginning of the devil. His first act was sin. That is probably doubtful, for He seems to have fallen. (3) From the beginning of the devil's rebellion. He sinned when He first rebelled and has kept it up. (4) From the beginning of the world. (5) From the beginning of the human race.

It is not easy to decide which of the above John had in mind; however, his major point is that sin has always been related to the devil. The two go together. Therefore, if a person lets sin become the ruling principle of his life, he is demonstrating his alignment with the devil. Like begets like.

Jesus came to do just the opposite. While the devil comes to work sin, Jesus came to **destroy** those works. The word **destroy** literally means to loose or set free (*luo*). It was used to refer to unloosening chains. The point is that Jesus came to unfasten the chains of sin that had captured us. He destroyed the works of the devil when he reconciled us to God through the cross. The authentic Christian continues to destroy the works of the devil in his own life as he purifies himself (v. 3), and practices righteousness (v. 7).

B. He's Compatible with the Father's Begetting, v. 9

No one who is born of God practices sin, because His seed abides in him; and he cannot sin, because he is born of God (3:9).

A Christian is a child of God (v. 1) not just by adoption, but also by birth. That's what Jesus meant when He said to Nicodemus, "You must be born again" (Jn. 3:3). The Greek word for "again" also means "from above." Jesus was stressing the fact that everyone who had sinned must be born *from above*. He needs to be **born of God**. God is in the begetting business; and changes result in the children of God that He begets. One change is that we don't continue allowing sin to be the ruling principle in our lives.

In this verse are two situations and two causes:

The Situation	The Cause (*hoti*)
No one practices sin	God's seed abides in him
He cannot sin	Born of God

That sounds as if the Christian *never* sins. But John was not saying that at all. He was stressing what he had already stressed—that *we aren't perfectly sinless, but we are not persistently sinning*. Though he had already made that clear, he revealed the *reason* the Christain's life-style isn't one of sin. The reason is because God's **seed** lives inside the Christian.

What is the **seed**? The word for "seed" is the Greek word *sperma* from which we get our English word sperm. It is accurate to say that God's sperm lives inside the Christian. That's why John said the Christian was

born of God. But just what is this *sperma* of God? The word is used in various ways: (1) The Word of God (James 1:18; I Pet. 1:23), (2) Family relationship—past geneology (Gal. 3:16, 29; Luke 1:55; John 8:33, 37). (3) In this context it seems to refer to the presence of the Holy Spirit. (See v. 24 and John 3:5-8.)

God uses His Word to plant the seed of His Spirit in us. The result is that we become partakers of the divine nature, "For by these He has granted to us His precious and magnificent promises, in order that by them you might become partakers of the divine nature, having escaped the corruption that is in the world by lust" (II Pet. 1:4).

The authentic Christian is born of God with His Spirit, and the fruit of the Spirit is not the works of the flesh (Gal. 5:16-25). It is unfortunate that some have used this verse to claim that the Christian *never* sins. If John intended to say that, he would not have used the present tense verb. The present tense verb in the Greek stresses an on-going continuous action—an habitual life-style. The Christian doesn't habitually sin.

But what did John mean when he said, **and he cannot sin?** Here are several explanations people have used to try to explain that:

1. The sins a Christian *cannot* do are the biggies—the "mortal" sins. But God has never catalogued sins into "big" or "small" ones.
2. God will not see a lawless deed as "sin" when a Christian does it. That doesn't square with the New Testament Scriptures. Paul made it clear that Christians do sin and that the acts are seen as such (Gal. 6:1).
3. The Christian has two natures living in him—the old nature and the new nature. When he sins, it isn't the new nature in him that's sinning but the old nature. So it isn't the "Christian" aspect but the "unchristian" aspect that's sinning. No! When a *person* sins, the *whole* person is involved.
4. This is an "ideal" to shoot for. John wrote fiction *not* fact. No! That's not the answer either.
5. This refers to only willful sins. A Christian never commits a willful sin. Oh? Most of our sins are willful. We *want* to do them, and we do them out of our desires. In fact, we are tempted when we are lured and enticed by our own desires (James 1:14).
6. John was speaking about habitual persistent sin. This is the answer. John used the present tense with the verbs **cannot** and **sin.** The idea is that the Christian is not continually able to keep on sinning because of his new nature. God's seed lives in him, and *that* seed produces a different kind of fruit than Satan's.

When a seed is planted what does it do? It grows. What does it produce? Fruit after its own kind. That's what God's seed is doing in us. It is gradually and daily transforming us into godliness (II Cor. 3:18). God gives us time to grow, not to continually sin. The Christian's behavior expresses the Father's begetting; and the longer he lives and the more mature he becomes, the more closely he resembles God's life-style.

III. An Accurate Confirmation, v. 10

By this the children of God and the children of the devil are obvious; any one who does not practice righteousness is not of God, nor the one who does not love his brother (3:10).

In this verse John summed up what he had said in verse four. Both the artificial Christian and the authentic Christian are known by their fruits. Each demonstrates whom he belongs to. The habitual sinner belongs to the devil (John 8:44; Acts 13:10; Eph. 2:3). The habitual doer of righteousness belongs to God. Our parent is either the devilish one or the divine one; we can't have it both ways. Each of us has the responsibility of choosing which parent we want.

Which parent do you want? Do you want to wallow in sin or walk in the Savior? Before deciding to remain in sin, you'd better review what John wrote about it. Here is another look at the preceding verses from another angle:

1. Sin's definition - lawlessness, v. 4
2. Sin's deeds - destroys Christ's work, v. 5
3. Sin's departure - does not associate with Christ, v. 6
4. Sin's derivation - the devil, v. 8
5. Sin's destruction - the seed of God, v. 9
6. Sin's destiny - the same as the devil, v. 10 (See Rev. 20:13-15).

Each of us has the responsibility to demonstrate whom we belong to by the way we live. The Devil is characterized by selfishness expressed in hate. He loves no one. God is characterized by unselfishness expressed in love. Thus the child of God loves his brothers. The proof is in the practice. How's your love-life? We'll look at that next.

QUESTIONS FOR DISCUSSION:

1. List ways to spot an antichrist.
2. How can 3:6, 9 stand alongside of 1:8?
3. If a Christian died in the act of a sin, would he be saved or lost?
4. How is loving one another related to loving God?
5. How did Christ take away sin?
6. How can we keep away sin?
7. Relate practicing righteousness and loving others.
8. Relate lawlessness and hating others.

Lesson Eight
(3:11-24)

HOW'S YOUR LOVE LIFE?

I. The Commandment, v. 11
II. The Contrast, vv. 12-15
   A. With Cain, v. 12
   B. With the World, v. 13
   C. With Death, v. 14
   D. With Hatred, v. 15
III. The Comparison, v. 16
IV. The Compassionate Cost, v. 17
V. The Challenge, v. 18
VI. The Confidence, vv. 19-24
   A. In His Position, v. 19
   B. With God's Persuasion, v. 20
   C. In Prayers, vv. 21-23
   D. With Christ's Presence, v. 24

I. *The Commandment, v. 11*

For this is the message which you have heard from the beginning, that we should love one another (3:11).

THIRTEEN LESSONS ON I, II AND III JOHN

In verse 10, John had made the connection that practicing righteousness and loving the brothers is the same. If that is so, then sinning and hating are related. That's why after John discussed sinning and not sinning (vv. 4-10), he discussed loving and not loving (vv. 11-24).

How are the two related? Righteousness and sin are *principles,* while love and hatred are *practices* that come from those principles. As the non-Christian's practice of sinning is rooted to a beginning (v. 8), so the Christian's practice of loving is rooted to a beginning. This verse reminds us of the first few verses of this writing which discuss Jesus. Notice the connection:

1:1-5 (Jesus)	3:11 (love)
message, v. 5	message,
have heard, v. 1	have heard
from the	from the
beginning, v. 1	beginning

The point of this literary connection is that Jesus is both the incarnation and example of love. Jesus came loving people and commanded His disciples to follow Him. As a tree can be identified partly by its fruit, so a Christian can be identified partly by his love life. A Christian can evaluate his love life by some of the tests John gave in this section: Can it be constrasted with Cain's, or is it like Cain's (v. 12)? Is it in conflict with the world (v. 13)? Does it enhance life (v. 14)? Does it ignore another (v. 15)? Does it compare with Christ's love (vv. 17, 18)? Does it give the Christian confidence to live by and to die by (vv. 19-24)? We will briefly look at those tests.

II. *The Contrast,* vv. 12-15
   A. *With Cain*

Not as Cain who was of the evil one, and slew his brother. And for what reason did he slay him? Because his deeds were evil, and his brother's were righteous (3:12).

Both Cain and Abel had brought offerings to the Lord (Gen. 4:3-4); however, God had regard for Abel's but not Cain's. There has been much speculation as to why one was accepted while the other was rejected. Some have said that God wanted a blood sacrifice and not a grain sacrifice (Abel was an animal keeper while Cain was a grain farmer); however, there is no biblical basis for that suggestion. Later God commanded both animal and cereal offerings. God is not prejudiced against a person's occupation.

The best clues for the acceptance and rejection seem to be the comparison of Gen. 4:4 and Heb. 11:4:

CHAPTER 3   I JOHN 3:11-24

Gen. 4:4	Heb. 11:4
And Abel on his part also brought of the firstlings of his flock and of their fat portions.	By faith Abel offered to God a better sacrifice than Cain . . .

Two verses later in the Hebrews account we read, "And without faith it is impossible to please Him, for he who comes to God must believe that He is, and that He is a rewarder of those who seek Him" (Heb. 11:6).

It seems that Abel expressed faith by his offering while Cain didn't. But what kind of offering expressed faith? It was an offering of the *firstlings* and of their fat portions. Notice Abel gave in the plural (firstlings and portions). He gave the first and the best to God. That takes faith. The common sense approach is to keep the best for further breeding. But God has always asked for the best from us in order to manifest faith in His blessings, not in our logical manipulations. Abel believed that if he gave away his first and finest that God would reward him (Heb. 11:6). But evidently Cain kept the first and finest for a later bumper crop. He lacked faith in God.

The church can learn from the example of these two brothers. It isn't enough to just be doing things. The church must step out on faith. Too often we want to see how things are going to turn out before we make decisions. Paul commended the church at Thessalonica for their "walk of faith" (I Thess. 1:3).

Cain did not have to lock himself into negative living by that one act; however, he didn't bounce back. He saw that his brother was a competitor so he decided to kill him. The word used here for **slew** literally means to "cut the throat." Cain had never seen a person die. The only thing he had seen die was the animals. And so he did to his brother what he had observed his brother do to animals. He cut his jugular vein. Cain took a holy method (cut the throat for sacrifice) and used it in an unholy way.

There are many lessons we can learn from this Cain-Abel incident. Here are a few:

1. There is power in the suggestion of sight. Cain had seen the slaughtering of animals and killed his brother in the same way. Today, too many people are entertained each evening by watching people kill, mutilate, and maul other people—for hours. Before a child reaches the age of 5 years old he will spend more time watching television than a college student spends in the classroom in 4 years. Sometime ago a survey of the content of prime time programs on the three major networks was taken. Between 3 PM and 11 PM were aired 113 stabbings, 92 shootings, 168 beatings, 9 stranglings, and 179 specific acts of violence. If we watch it, we may practice it.

2. There is destructive power in jealousy. Cain kept score. Do we? When we do, we slip into jealousy. Jealousy moves us into hatred. And hatred moves us into murder. There are different ways to kill a person. We might not "cut his throat," but we might undercut his reputation by slander. Paul wrote, "But if we bite and devour one another, take care lest you be consumed by one another" (Gal. 5:15). Both "biting and devouring" and "cutting the throat" were done to animals. If we don't love as God does, we will eventually live like animals. We are fellow-people, not fellow-animals. And we should live like it.
3. Being in the same family doesn't guarantee security. Today more murders in the United States are committed by family members than by anyone else. Christian doctrine and Christian deeds must, first of all, be applied at home.

But there is another kind of "brotherly" murder that's going on today. It's the killing that's going on within the family of God — one of GOD'S children murdering another of God's children. It happens because of the hatreds manufactured because of the barriers erected in denominationalism. People in one group who hate people in another group are walking in the sandals of Cain. And that's the opposite attitude of John's outlook as he began this writing — "that you may have fellowship with us" (1:4).

B. *With the World,* v. 13

Do not marvel, brethren, if the world hates you (3:13).

How are you getting along with the world these days? There is a new faddish teaching in Christianity today that goes something like this: "Live a Christian life, and everything will be great." And then when things go sour, people marvel — "How could *that* happen to me? I've done so much for God." John said, "Don't marvel. God never promised us a rose garden. He promised us hatred." What? That's right. You love the way Christ loved, and the world will hate you as it hated Him. The world will hate us for the same reason Cain hated Abel — jealousy.

The word "hate" doesn't just mean despise, it also means neglect. It's tough to be neglected. I'm amazed how some Christians can't understand it when the world doesn't come in great crowds to hear them or reward them. It then becomes tempting to try to lure the world. Our job is to love the brothers, not to lure the world to love us. If we love the brothers, many in the world will want to come out of it into the family of God. Jesus promised it (John 17:21). We should believe it.

C. *With Death,* v. 14

We know that we have passed out of death into life, because we love the brethren. He who does not love abides in death (3:14).

CHAPTER 3   I JOHN 3:11-24

One of the practical evidences that the Christian has been transferred from the kingdom of Satan to the kingdom of God's Son is his love life. The person who is not loving his brother as an habitual pattern of his life is just kidding himself if he claims to be a Christian. A real Christian loves. A change of position (with Christ) will change his practices (love).

The Bible has much to say about the person who is always causing strife. Jude made it clear that such a person is "devoid of the Spirit" (Jude 19). And why not? For the fruit of the Spirit begins with love (Gal. 5:22). Paul wrote that a factious person should be rejected from the fellowship after a second warning (Titus 3:10-11). Why? Because a genuine Christian loves. To allow the counterfeit to remain is to communicate to him that he has **passed out of death into life** when he really hasn't. To pass into life is to pass into a life of love. To not be loving is to be remaining in death, the old kingdom of Satan, regardless of how many times the person has been baptized, how many perfect attendance pins he has, or how much of the Bible he has memorized. To be in the life and not to love is an impossibility. How's your love life?

D. With Hatred, v. 15

Everyone who hates his brother is a murderer; and you know that no murderer has eternal life abiding in him (3:15).

The person who doesn't love hates: there is no middle ground. A person is either alive or dead; he either loves or hates. There's no such thing as a fence straddler on these essential issues.

It's so easy to read about Cain and yell, "Mafia." We wouldn't *murder!* But John reminded his readers that hating is murdering. The only difference between the two is the actual act. Hating is the root; murdering is the fruit. Both share the same results, alienation. Both will share the same eternal consequences, condemnation.

III. The Comparison, v. 16

We know love by this, that He laid down His life for us; and we ought to lay down our lives for the brethren (3:16).

It's not enough to show the opposite of love by rehearsing the Cain-Abel incident. In addition to knowing what to avoid, the Christian needs a model of what to imitate if he is to demonstrate love. For love can mean many different things to different people, and the difference gets more complex in different cultures.

However, there is one model of love that is transcultural and transtemporal. That model is Jesus. If you really want to KNOW what love is, look at Jesus. Instead of being a taker of life as Cain was, Jesus was a giver of life. Here's a brief comparison of Cain and Christ.

THIRTEEN LESSONS ON I, II AND III JOHN

Cain (Gen. 4)	Christ
brought an inferior offering	brought a superior offering
gave for self praise	gave for God's praise
angry with God	submitted to God
didn't master sin	mastered sin
had zeal against his brother	has zeal for his brother
was jealous	was joyous
took another's life	gave his own life
gave with competitive spirit	gave with substitutionary spirit
asked, "Am I my brother's keeper?"	lived as His brother's keeper
was cursed	was glorified

However, it isn't enough just to note that a person gave His life for another. We need to look at the motivation behind it. Was He forced to do so against His personal wish? Did He do it to become a hero? Did He do it by accident? Did He do it to repay a debt? Jesus' love is perfect not only because of *what* He did, but *why* He did it and *for whom* He did it.

He gave His life *voluntarily*. He confessed, "No one has taken it away from me, but I lay it down on my own initiative . . ." (John 10:18). He didn't do it for selfish reasons, but totally for the benefit of others — ". . . for the sheep" (John 10:11). He had the power to not lay down His life, for he could have had 72,000 angels defend Him when a few men came to arrest Him (Matt. 26:53). But He didn't call for reinforcements. He died as our substitute for our benefit. That's the significance of the words **for us**: the word **for** (*huper*) stresses a beneficial substitute. And He did it for people who didn't like Him — "But God demonstrates His own love toward us, in that while we were yet sinners, Christ died for us" (Romans 5:8). Jesus once said, "Greater love has no one than this, that one lay down his life for his friends" (John 15:13). But the irony of it is that He Himself had greater love than that, because He gave His life for His enemies. No wonder He is the perfect model for love. Do you want to know love? Then know Jesus!

It is only because of His death **for us** that we can live forever with Him. Therefore, we have become debtors to pass on that love to others. **We ought** stresses the obligations of a debt. We are to always be a living I.O.U. Paul put it this way, "Owe nothing to anyone except to love one another . . ." (Rom. 13:8). That means we are never to get that debt paid off. But how do we love another? The same way Jesus did — **to lay down our lives for the brethren.**

But one word here makes our love a notch lower than Jesus' love. Jesus died for His *enemies*. John says we are to lay down our lives for the *brethren*. But be careful with this. John is stressing where to *start*, not where to finish. Elsewhere we read that we are to also love our enemies

(Matt. 5:43-48). We are also to do for our enemies what John suggested in the next verse we are to do for our brothers (Rom. 12:20-21). However, our love will not branch out to our enemies unless we, first of all, love our brothers. Loving our brothers is the "boot-camp" for our love, not the "front lines" of it, nor the totality of it. Remember, we are to love *just as* Jesus loved. And His circle of love was wide enough to include everyone. Paul prayed that ours would also become that wide (Eph. 3:14-21).

Does **to lay down our lives** mean we too must go to the cross? Absolutely! Jesus made it clear that His disciples must take up their cross:

> Then Jesus said to His disciples, "If anyone wishes to come after Me, let him deny himself, and take up His cross, and follow Me. For whoever wishes to save his life shall lose it; but whoever loses his life for my sake shall find it. For what will a man be profited, if he gains the whole world, and forfeits his soul?" (Matt. 16:24-26).

> Whoever does not carry his own cross and come after Me cannot be My disciple (Luke 14:27).

But what does it mean to take up a cross? It has become somewhat popular to talk about a sickness or tragedy as "bearing my cross." But the New Testament *never* refers to that as cross bearing. Others say, "My cross is my children, wife, or husband!" Sorry! They are not crosses.

The cross in the New Testament always referred to a crucifixion. To take up your cross is to do what Jesus did — voluntarily crucify selfishness. That's why the words "deny self" and "take up his cross" are found in the same sentence (Matt. 16:24; Mark 8:34; Luke 9:23). We don't nail our literal body to a literal cross, but we do die to selfishness and arise to an unselfish life of love.

This event of transformation begins when we go through the death, burial, and resurrection at baptism (Romans 6), but it is to continue daily. Jesus said, "If anyone wishes to come after me, let him deny himself, and take up his cross *daily*, and follow me." Although the *initial* death to self and burial of that in baptism happens only once, the new life goes on *daily*. That's why Paul said that he was "always carrying about in the body the dying of Jesus, that the life of Jesus also may be manifested in our body" (II Cor. 4:10). The "dying of Jesus" is the denial of selfishness, which is doing what we do just for the benefit of self. The "life of Jesus" is the caring for other people's needs. That's what is to be "manifested in our body." That's love incarnated today. Christ's love transforms our compassion into caring activities that costs us our possessions.

IV. *The Compassionate Cost,* v. 17

> **But whoever has the world's goods, and beholds his brother in need and closes his heart against him, how does the love of God abide in him? (3:17).**

THIRTEEN LESSONS ON I, II AND III JOHN

No person lays down his life for another without laying down his possessions to meet the needs of the other. We are just kidding ourselves if we think we live for others but will not give up our livelihood to provide for another. That's the acid test of love.

This world is made up of the haves and the have-nots. God is the God of both (Prov. 22:2). And He loves both. **Whoever has the world's goods** has a responsibility to act like God acts with His possessions—share them. The word for **world's goods** (*bios*) stresses the dividends we have gained by investing our lives in work. A Christian is to work partly to provide for himself (II Thess. 3:10); to provide for his family, which includes his aged parents (I Tim. 5:8); to provide for world evangelism (I Cor. 9:9-14; Phil. 4:15-17); and to provide for another in physical need (Eph. 4:28; I Tim. 6:17-19; II Cor. 8-9; Acts 2:44-45; 4:36-37). Every Christian ought to use his finances in a way that includes all four of these. To neglect one while emphasizing another is immature. Jesus criticized the Pharisees for doing that (Matt. 15:1-9).

It is easy to neglect benevolent work if we are heavily supporting evangelistic work. That's why the New Testament often stresses our benevolence. God knows that we can so easily overlook it. Someone may say, "There you go again, stressing money. All the church is concerned about is my finances." Sorry folks! That's not correct. To react like that is simply a confession that that's all *you* are concerned about. The church isn't interested in your finances, but your future. She isn't interested in your savings, but in your salvation. However, the two are directly related. If you doubt that, read and study these Scriptures: Matthew 25:31-46; Luke 10:25-37; 12:13-21; 16:19-31; James 2:14-26.

The person who will not care outwardly is the person who doesn't have compassion inwardly, and he **closes his heart.** The word **heart** here is literally the word "bowels." It refers to "the pit of the stomach" where compassion is felt when a person sees another in need. If that doesn't happen, then Christ isn't living inside; for the indwelling Christ changes the inside of a person. And if the inside hasn't changed, the **love of God** isn't abiding in that person.

The **love of God** could refer to our love for God or God's love for us. It probably refers to the fact that we really don't love God if we don't care for His people. John made that point clear in the next chapter (I John 4:20).

The person who closes up his heart is just like Cain. The miser is like the murderer. The stingy one is the slaughterer of another. John made it clear that the genuine Christian can't get off the hook by saying, "I don't really *hate* him: I'm just not going to use my finances to help take care of him." The two attitudes are the same.

To lay down our lives involves giving up what is valuable to us for others, because with our changed view those people now have more value.

CHAPTER 3   I JOHN 3:11-24

V. *The Challenge,* v. 18

Little children let us not love with word or with tongue, but in deed and truth (3:18).

John's challenge is for Christians (**little children**) to move love out of just saying the three words, "I love you," to doing something. It has become rather popular for some worshippers to turn to the persons around them and say, "I love you." That cute exercise doesn't impress God. Love isn't captured in words, but in works. I've had many people tell me they love me because of the manipulation of the worship leader, but not one has ever come to me afterwards and asked if I had any needs.

We can either love in tongue or in truth. To love in tongue is to say the words; to love in truth is to do the deeds. Isn't it interesting that Jesus never once said to anyone, "I love you"? He just demonstrated it. This isn't to suggest that we should never use the words. But it is to suggest that we should not *word* it, if we don't *work* it. That's the challenge — *declare* it by *doing* it. Then we know that our lives are really manifesting Jesus' life.

VI. *The Confidence,* vv. 19-24

We shall know by this that we are of the truth, and shall assure our heart before Him, in whatever our heart condemns us; for God is greater than our heart, and knows all things. Beloved, if our heart does not condemn us, we have confidence before God; and whatever we ask we receive from Him, because we keep his commandments and do the things that are pleasing in his sight. And this is his commandment, that we believe in the name of His Son Jesus Christ and love one another, just as He commanded us. And the one who keeps His commandments abides in Him, and He in them. And we know by this that He abides in us, by the Spirit which He has given us (3:19-24).

The loving in deed and truth gives the Christian confidence in this world. It gives us confidence about many facets of Christianity:

A. *In His Position,* v. 19

It is by loving the way Jesus loved that we can know **we are of the truth.** To be **of the truth** is to be of Jesus who is the truth (John 14:6). The lover can be confident that his practice of love comes from his position in the Lord.

B. *With God's Persuasion,* v. 20

Our hearts often tell us that we are falling short of being Christ's disciples. Satan tries to discourage us. That often causes us to turn

79

inwardly and spend an unhealthy amount of time in introspection. But the one who is really loving can know that God understands us and is **greater than our heart.** He's so great that He forgives (20-21), gives (v. 22), and is our companion (23-24). The person who is really loving is never totally satisfied with what he is doing. He always wants to do more. Such a person may feel guilty when he buys anything for himself. But God **knows all things.** He knows that we love by providing for others. He knows that the widow's mite may express more love than Wall Street's millions. Our confidence is not in how much we give in comparison to others but in God who knows us and loves us.

C. *In Prayers*, vv. 21-23

The person who loves as Christ loved has confidence in prayers because his prayers are the fruit of the correct rootage — **because we keep His commandments and do the things that are pleasing in His sight.** His commandments are summed up in only two: **believe in the name of His Son Jesus Christ** and **love one another.** Both of those relate. For to believe in the **name** of Jesus is to have confidence in Him as a person and what He did. What did He do? He loved. He gave Himself up for others. So to really believe in Him is to also **love one another.** To really **love one another** is to do for them **the things that are pleasing in His sight.** And when that is our life-style, we can be confident in prayer. Why? Because our prayers are uttered unselfishly.

This verse cannot be taken out of its context of loving others, and then made to say that anything that anyone asks will be granted. Absolutely not! Elsewhere we read a lot about the conditions of answered prayers. Prayers are answered when they are asked for unselfish purposes (James 4:1-3), according to God's will (John 15:7), in Christ's name (John 16:23-24), while obeying His commandments, and by doing what pleases God (I John 3:22). It is the person who imitates Christ's love (I John 3:16-18) that prays like that. For instance — he prays for a pay raise, so he will have more to share. He prays for long life, so he will have more time to help others. He prays for health, so he will have more money and strength available to let the life of Christ be manifested in his life.

D. *With Christ's Presence*, v. 24

The person who loves as Christ loved has the assurance that Christ abides in Him, for that's the only way a person can love daily. In this section, his confidence began with the idea that he himself was in Christ **(in the truth** — v. 19) and concluded with the assurance that Christ is in Him. That's the unity of the real Christian. The fellowship is two-way. Christ is in us **by the Spirit that He has given us.** That Spirit is the extended earthly presence of deity. We can love because God who is love abides in us: "Our" love is really His love expressing itself through the availability of our bodies. "Our" functions of love are really the Spirit's fruit (Gal. 5:22).

CHAPTER 3   I JOHN 3:11-24

Make it your habit to love, and you can have confidence in your position (v. 19), with God's persuasion (v. 20), in your prayers (v. 21-22), and with Christ's presence (v. 24). What a blessing it is to love!

QUESTIONS FOR DISCUSSION:
1. List specific instances in which you think Christian love (a) was not or (b) was manifested to people in your community.
2. What are some ways to "kill" a brother?
3. The word "hate" can mean to treat someone as "second rate." List ways to treat fellow Christians as (a) "second rate," (b) "first rate."
4. List the areas of ministry in which (a) you (b) your classs (c) your congregation is "laying down the life" for the brethren.
5. List ways #4 could be expanded.
6. How much of your personal giving is specifically designated for benevolence? Why or why not?
7. How is keeping God's commandments related to loving one another?

Part Five

LIFE IN THE SPIRIT

IX. Professing the Divine Lord, 4:1-6
X. Practicing the Divine Life, 4:7 — 5:5

Immediately after John mentioned that Christians have been given the Holy Spirit (3:24), he discussed what it meant to live in the Spirit. It involves the right kind of confession (in the Lord) and the right kind of conduct (in the love). The two cannot be separated. Our practices are rooted in whom we profess.

Lesson Nine
(4:1-6)

Professing the Divine Lord

I. The Call for Testing the "Profession," 4:1
II. A Criterion for Testing, 4:2-6
   A. The Confession of the Speaker, 4:2-3
      1. When It's from the Holy Spirit, 4:2
      2. When It's not from the Holy Spirit, 4:3
   B. The Character of the Hearers, 4:4-6
      1. Who the Conquerors Are, 4:4
      2. Who the Conquered Are, 4:5
      3. What the Conflict Is; 4:6

I. *The Call for Testing*

Beloved, do not believe every spirit, but test the spirits to see whether they are from God; because many false prophets have gone out into the world (4:1).

One of the distinguishing marks of a Christian is that he is a person who trusts. However, John warned his readers against turning belief into gullibility. Because Christians are **beloved** by God doesn't mean they can't be beguiled by the devil. The Galatian Christians experienced that bewitching activity rather early in their new lives (Gal. 1:6; 3:1). And

CHAPTER 4   I JOHN 4:1-6

evidently John realized that many Christians toward the end of the first century were also being tempted to follow false teachings that were disguised as spiritual truth.

All of the warnings to Christians in the New Testament spotlight the truth that it is possible for the Christians to fall. The Devil knows that. That's why he keeps his guns turned on the Christian as well as the non-Christian—"therefore let him who thinks he stands take heed lest he fall" (I Cor. 10:12). The Christian is repeatedly commanded to stay alert, be watchful, flee temptation, repent, endure, and overcome. The Christian's falling away can always be traced to some false teaching to which he has exposed his mind, for what we continually pour into our minds will eventually flow out of our lives. The Christian must censure his mental intake. A Christian's listening to anything can easily slip into gullibility to believe anything.

John gave the responsibility to **test the spirits** to the **beloved,** not to a board. As no Christian is exempt from living the truth, neither is he exempt from evaluating what is truth. It can't be done by proxy. It has to be done personally.

One of the current tragedies in Christianity is that we have too easily rested our doctrinal position upon a creedal statement that someone else has designed without working through an evaluative process ourselves. That kind of mentality will perpetuate denominational lines. When that happens, tradition is elevated to truth. The Jews did it (Mark 7:1-8), and we do it today.

Since Christians have the capacity to believe, we also have both a positive and negative command about the way we utilize that capacity. We saw the positive command in 3:23, "And this is His commandment, that we believe in the name of His Son Jesus Christ. . . ." Now we see the negative command, **"Do not believe every spirit."** This is not an option, but an obligation. It must be taken seriously.

Why would John give such a command? Because of the reality of other spirits besides the Holy Spirit in the world. There is only one Spirit of truth—the Holy Spirit (4:6; John 14:17). Every other spirit is a spirit of error, even though it might inspire someone to say things which are accurate. The final goal of this latter spirit is deception that will turn people away from God. The fact that other spirits do exist is clear in the New Testament (Matt. 12:22-45; Mark 1:23-27; 3:11; 5:2-20; 6:7; 7:25; 9:17-29; Acts 5:16; 8:7; 16:16-18; 19:16; I Cor. 2:12; 12:10; Eph. 2:2; I Tim. 4:1; Rev. 16:13).

Thus "spiritual" influences are not always "godly" influences. The unholy spirits use all sorts of gimmicks to disciple people to their teachings. They will quote Scripture, verbally confess Jesus as the Son of God, perform miracles, use the phrase "in the name of Jesus," disguise themselves as angels of light, and prophesy events of the future. It's a strong temptation to believe such spirits, but Christians are not to be dazzled by the sensational.

The evil spirits can look very sincere in their zeal for missions, evangelism, education, and benevolent ministries. But we should not be fooled into thinking that just because somebody has one or all of these interests that he is from God. As no saint is exempt from testing the spirits, so no speaker is exempt from being tested.

And no wonder, for even Satan disguises himself as an angel of light. Therefore it is not surprising if his servants also disguise themselves as servants of righteousness; whose end shall be according to their deeds (II Cor. 11:14-15).

A person's popularity, theological training, or activities do not exclude him from Satan's influence. Even one of the apostles was lured into becoming an instrument of Satan. It's a mark of spiritual maturity to not believe every spirit. If we aren't to believe them all, what are we to do? We are to test them, **do not belive . . . but test** is John's command. Both aspects of that command are to be obeyed.

The word **test** (*dokimazo*) is an interesting word. It refers to testing something in order to determine its character. The Greek word has the same root as the Greek word for character (*dokime*). So this is a character-test. It was the word used to describe the evaluation of the character or genuineness of metals.

But *what* do we test about spirits? We test their source — **to see whether they are from God.** Any spirit comes from either a diabolical or divine source. But *how* does a person test spirits? Aren't spirits invisible? Yes and no. Spirits are invisible, but they always manifest themselves through physical bodies. They love to work through **false prophets.** So we can test spirits **because many false prophets have gone out into the world:** and we can certainly see, hear, and touch prophets. Thus we test the spirits by testing the speaker who claims to be uttering the messages of God.

Biblically, **prophets** are always inspired people. But they are not always inspired by God. Behind every **prophet**, there is a spirit. The question is which kind of spirit? God used **prophets** as did the devil. In fact, the devil keeps an active recruiting program. There were not just *some* false prophets in the world in John's day, but **many**. And they are still around today.

Here's an interesting truth. God does not have prophets in the world today, but the devil does. God is not *inspiring* people to speak His Words as He did in the Old Testament days. His prophets wrote down what God inspired them to say. Eventually, God directed His people through

CHAPTER 4   I JOHN 4:1-6

the inspired written Word. False prophets who continued could be checked partly by whether or not their teachings squared with the written Word of God.

With the coming of the New Covenant, God again used inspired people to utter His Word. They also wrote down God's teachings, and the church is built upon that foundation (Eph. 2:20). False prophets today can be tested partly by whether or not their teachings square with the New Testament writings.

But we must all be extremely cautious at this point. Just because a person's teachings do not *completely* square with all the New Testament doesn't mean that he is automatically a false prophet. He could be speaking from a misunderstanding of the text, not from the inspiration of an unholy spirit. Every Christian grows in his understanding. And we must allow for that growth. It is too tempting to label anyone who doesn't cross all his doctrinal "T's" the way we do as a "false prophet." Some things I thought I understood correctly a few years ago, I now realize that I didn't. A person who teaches an erroneous concept about a New Testament truth may be of God although a particular teaching is not. I doubt that any of us perfectly teach perfect truths. We are all learning.

If that is true, then is there any test that stands above all others for testing the spirits behind the speakers? Yes, there is. It is the Christological test. What is the speaker's position about Jesus? We will look at that text next.

II. *A Criterion for Testing,* 4:2, 3
   A. *The Confession of the Speaker,* 4:2, 3
      1. *When It's from the Holy Spirit,* v. 2

By this you know the Spirit of God: every spirit that confesses that Jesus Christ has come in the flesh is from God (4:2).

Every false prophet will fail the test of confessing Jesus Christ, for that confession comes from the Holy Spirit. And the Holy Spirit does not inspire the antichrists.

To confess Jesus Christ involves much more than saying words about Jesus. In fact, the word "that" — **confesses** *that* **Jesus Christ** — is not in the Greek. The Christian is not just to confess facts about Jesus, but confess Him. There is a big difference between the two. A contemporary illustration should demonstrate the difference between confessing a fact about a person and confessing the person: I am writing this during a presidential election year. President Jimmy Carter is finishing his first term in office. If at the Republican nominating convention, the presider asked every person present who believed the fact that Jimmy Carter is the President of the United States to come forward and confess that fact, they *all* would be able to do that. But if the presider asked for those who would commit their allegiance to Jimmy Carter to confess that commitment, the crowd at the front would diminish.

Confessing Jesus always involves the commitment of the life to Jesus. It is never just the saying of words. The demons could say the words that Jesus was the Son of God (Mark 1:24; 3:11; 5:7; Acts 16:17; 19:15). It's one thing to let Jesus be on the lips, but its another thing to let Jesus be in the life (Matt. 7:21-23; Luke 6:46).

The Christian is confessing that **Jesus Christ has come in the flesh.** That covers a lot of commitment to Jesus. It means we are committed to His *pre-existent state, and* to His *on-going results* in our lives, for the verb's perfect tense **has come** stresses *abiding results.* It means that the one who lived in the flesh once will still live in flesh today. He abides in our flesh.

It means that we are committed to his humanity . . . **in the flesh;** thus He is *our model* for human living. To confess **Jesus** also means we are committed to *His saving work,* because the word "Jesus" means "Savior." This seven word confession also means that we are committed to *His divinity* which is spotlighted in the word **Christ.** He is God's anointed Messiah. There is no other. Thus He is *our Lord and King.* He speaks and we obey.

Commitment to this confession must be measured by everything else John wrote. Are we fellowshipping with Jesus and His people? Are we confessing sin? Are we loving others? Have we rejected sin as an habitual life-style? Are we obeying His commandments? Are we listening to truth?

2. When It's Not from the Holy Spirit, 4:3

And every spirit that does not confess Jesus is not from God; and this is the spirit of the antichrist, of which you have heard that it is coming, and now it is already in the world (4:3).

The one who speaks "spiritual truths" but doesn't confess Jesus in all that's involved in that commitment is being used by the spirit of the antichrist. But remember it isn't enough for a person to just say he believes in Jesus. The question is — which Jesus?

In John's day the heretical philosophers of Gnosticism believed in a man Jesus but not the pre-existent Jesus who was divine, eternal, and became flesh. There were two ideas about Jesus which they popularized. One was that Jesus was just one of God's many creations in a long line of creatures. Thus, He was a mere human being. Another idea was that the divine element of Jesus came on Him at baptism and left Him before He died. Both of those ideas about Jesus stood opposed to the truth of God who became flesh (John 1:11-14; Phil. 2:5-11). They were denying that the Messiah came in the flesh.

CHAPTER 4 I JOHN 4:1-6

To strip away either the humanity or the divinity of Jesus is to divide Him. So it isn't surprising that some ancient manuscripts read "every spirit that divides Christ is not from God." The word used for divide (*luo*) meant to destroy, set aside, sever. To dilute the "God in flesh" concept divides Jesus.

The spirit of the antichrist is always interested in watering down the doctrine about Jesus. And it's happening today through the teachings of many seminaries. It is now popularly taught that the Jesus we read about in the New Testament is not the factual Jesus, but a fictitious Jesus. The idea is that we are reading what people in the first century believed about Jesus or wanted to believe about Him, but not about the factual, historical Jesus Christ (form criticism). Another teaching is that we are not reading an inspired word about Jesus but the editorial slant of the individual writer (redaction criticism). Both teachings have successfully weakened ministerial students' commitment to the infallibility of Jesus' words and works.

Do you want to test the spirits behind a person's teaching? Then begin by asking him pointed questions about Jesus. You can also test what the teacher really believes about Jesus not only by what he says with his lips, but also by how he lives his life.

B. *The Character of the Hearers, 4:4-6*

1. *Who the Conquerors Are, 4:4*

You are from God, little children and have overcome them, because greater is He who is in you than he who is in the world (4:4).

After John exposed those who were of the antichrist's spirit, he immediately reminded his readers that they were not in that position. **You are from God,** the word **you** is emphasized in the Greek. John contrasted those who were not confessing Jesus (v. 3) with his readers who were confessing Jesus and living like it.

But why didn't his readers get duped by the wrong spirits? How have they **overcome** thus far? John reminded them why they haven't been beguiled — **greater is He that is in you, than he who is in the world.** No Christian needs to think that the unholy spirits in the world are stronger than the Holy One who abides in the Christian (3:24). They aren't! That's why they always fled in the presence of Jesus. No Christian has to give way to "the spirit that is now working in the sons of disobedience" (Eph. 2:2). No Christian has to become a servant to "the ruler of this world" (John 12:31); the Christian has already been delivered from that old kingdom (Col. 1:13). So for the Christian to say, "I *can't* resist" is ridiculous. The Christian possesses the powerful presence of God through the Holy Spirit. And the one Holy Spirit is stronger than millions of unholy spirits. The Christian has not overcome by his own strength. Because he has been transferred to a *new position* (in Christ), he has had transferred to him a *new power* (the Holy Spirit). Through the Spirit, he has overcome the continuing onslaught of false prophets who are trying to detour his commitment from Jesus (1-3). That's why John said, **you . . . have overcome them.** The Christian has also overcome the habitual immoralities of the world — and eventually hell.

By considering the other times the word "overcome" (*nikao*) was used in the New Testament, we can discover what we are to overcome:

The world	John 16:33; I John 5:4, 5
The judgment	Rev. 3:4
Evil	Rev. 12:21
The evil one	I John 2:13, 14
False Prophets	I John 4:4
Leaving first love	Rev. 2:4-7
Persecution	Rev. 2:10-11; 3:7-12
Perverted teaching	Rev. 2:13-17, 20-26
False reputation	Rev. 3:1-5
Luke-warmness	Rev. 3:15-21
Devil's accusations	Rev. 12:10-11
The beast	Rev. 15:2

In summary, the Christian should overcome inferior doctrine, inferior deeds, and inferior destiny.

But people have read too much into this verse. They have read that John taught that his readers could *never* give in to false teachers because of the indwelling Holy Spirit. That is not so. We must always keep on the alert with the whole armor of God. The privilege of God's Spirit living in us must be matched with the practice of our commitment to live for God. If Christians could never succumb to false teachings, John would not have commanded them to "believe not every spirit, but test the spirits." That's the Christian's responsibility. If the Christians didn't need that, John would not have written it to them. God did not waste His time by inspiring the apostles and prophets to write warnings to Christians unless they needed those warnings.

2. *Who the Conquered Are,* v. 5

They are from the world; therefore they speak as from the world, and the world listens to them (4:5).

There is a correspondence between the false prophets and their audience. They are both **from the world,** which means from the Kingdom of Satan. We have already seen one way to test the speakers — *by their confession* (v. 3). Now we see another way to test them — *by their crowd.* Who's paying attention to them? What's happening in their lives and through their lives? There is always a functional relationship between our mental input and our moral output. As birds of a feather stick together, so do the speakers and listeners of the world. Look at the crowd that remains committed to a speaker, and you can tell something about what he is teaching.

3. What the Conflict Is, v. 6

We are from God; he who knows God listens to us; he who is not from God does not listen to us. By this we know the spirit of truth and the spirit of error (4:6).

The Word of God not only attracts people, but also repels them. One way to test both teacher and students is by seeing how they match up with each other. A genuine Christian listens to Christian teaching. **We are from God; he who knows God listens to us.** But a counterfeit Christian will stay away, **he who is not from God does not listen to us.** That probably says something about church members who never show up!

John did not suggest that people of the world can never be evangelized because they will never listen. Oh no! The only way people can be converted is by hearing the Word (Rom. 10:13-17). However, the non-Christian will not make it a habit to keep listening (present tense). The word for **listens** (*akouo*) involves obeying. John is talking about applying the teaching, not just audibly listening to it.

John did not intend for this verse to be used as a club over fellow Christians. Just because a person will not listen and apply *everything* "we" teach doesn't mean he is a non-Christian. Christians have different opinions and must live graciously with each other with those opinions (Rom. 14, I Cor. 8). That's why there is so much talk in the New Testament about Christians being patient with each other. However, we are to listen to one another's teachings about the human-divine character of Jesus and about our love to each other.

Some suggest that John referred to only the apostles when he talked about people listening to **us.** That is an attractive idea since the church is to continue in the apostle's doctrine (Acts 2:42); however, John certainly did not intend for the words "we" and "us" to be restricted to the apostles in the rest of this chapter (vv. 7, 9, 10, 11, 12, 13, 14, 16, 17, 19, 21), so this line of reasoning is extremely weak — too weak to take very seriously.

There is a significant teaching in this verse that is easily overlooked. It is the relationship of **knows God** (present tense) and **listens to us** (present tense). Probably none of us has mastered knowing God. Every time we read His Word or hear His teachers we can usually learn something new about Him. He is inexhaustible.

Then how do we know Him? Always through someone else. We know Him through Jesus (John 14:7); but it doesn't end then, for Christians become a living epistle from Him to be read by others (II Cor. 3). People listen to us in order to know God. That's partly what it means to be His representatives (II Cor. 5:17-19). What an awesome responsibility we have. While people have not beheld God, they can observe something about Him through what we say (v. 6) and through how we love (v. 12).

The conflict between **the spirit of truth** which is the Holy Spirit (John 14:17; 15:26; 16:13), and the **spirit of error** which is the spirit of Satan (I Tim. 4:1) is seen in the speakers and in their audience. The acid test lies in what is being declared and what is being demonstrated.

Lips that declare love must be supported by lives that demonstrate love. John turned to that dimension next.

QUESTIONS FOR DISCUSSION:

1. Is it possible for someone without God's Spirit to love? (Check Matt. 5:46).
2. Discuss the implications of accepting Christ's divinity without His humanity.
3. Discuss the implications of accepting His humanity without His divinity.
4. Is just confessing that Jesus came in the flesh the only way to spot false prophets? Can false teachers say the right words?
5. What is involved in confessing?
6. How can we guard against being lured by false spirits?
7. What are some basic teachings of false spirits today?
8. What does it mean to "overcome the world"?

Lesson Ten
(4:7 — 5:5)

Practicing the Divine Life

I. The Cause of Love, vv. 7-8
II. The Character of God's Love, vv. 9-10
III. Our Obligation With God's Love, vv. 11-12
    A. The Responsibility, v. 11
    B. The Result, v. 12
IV. Some Certainties in Love, vv. 13-18
    A. Our Present Consolidation, vv. 13-16
    B. Our Future Confidence, vv. 17-18
V. The Sharing of God's Love, v. 19
VI. The Integrity of Love, vv. 20-21
    A. With Our Confession, v. 20
    B. With His Commandments, v. 21
VII. The Integration of Love, 5:1-5

It was only natural for John to progress from confessing the divine Lord to demonstrating the divine life, because Jesus came to *reshape* our living on earth as well as to *redeem* it for heaven. John summed up the divine life by one concept — love.

THIRTEEN LESSONS ON I, II AND III JOHN

At first glance, it looks as if John continued to repeat himself. He had already discussed love in 2:7-11 and 3:11-22. But in each section he introduces a different aspect about love. In a sense, each new section is a new phase that takes us a step beyond the preceding phases. Each step is more mature than the preceding step. The first phase introduced us to the fact that love is a command (2:7-11). The second phase introduced us to some do's and don'ts involved in the conduct of love (3:11-22). The third phase introduced us to the highest motivations for loving — love is the nature of God, manifests God's presence in us, demonstrates our unity with the Godhead, gives us confidence for the day of judgment, and cannot be isolated from other essential teachings in Christianity. The following chart pictures these steps.

THE ACCELERATING STEPS OF LOVE IN I JOHN

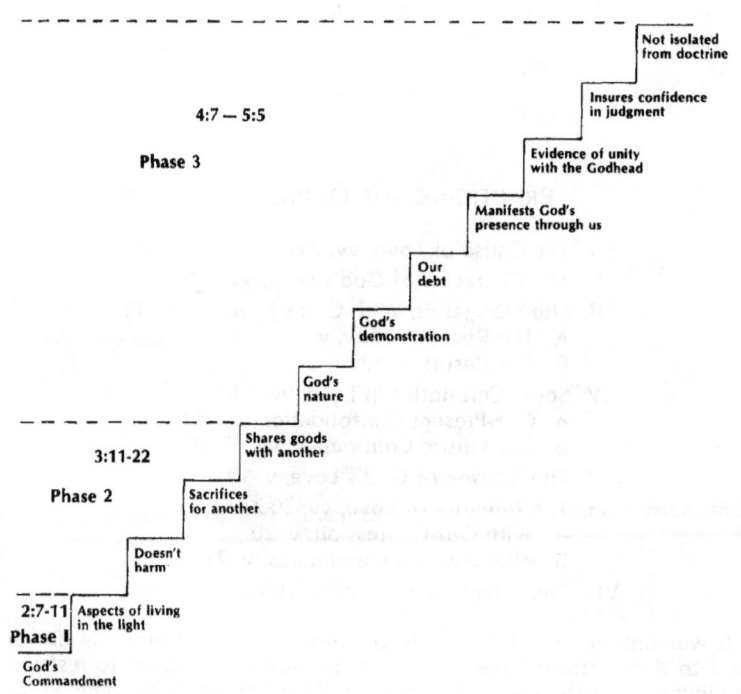

I. *The Cause of Love,* vv. 7-8

Beloved, let us love one another, for love is from God; and every one who loves is born of God and knows God. The one who does not love does not know God, for God is love (4:7-8).

John moved from listening (v. 6) to loving (v.7). What a natural move. We are to listen to one another partly to stimulate one another to love the way God wants us to love. That's one reason why we assemble together regularly (Hebrews 10:24-25). Paul dedicated much of his Christian life teaching people so that he might present them mature in Christ — "And we proclaim Him admonishing every man and teaching every man with all wisdom, that we may present every man complete in Christ" (Col. 1:28). The mark of maturity is that love might flow from a changed life — "But the goal of our instruction is love from a pure heart and a good conscience and a sincere faith" (I Tim. 1:5). We listen to love.

Tradition tells us that John spent his last years in Ephesus as an old man. When he was too feeble to walk to the assembly, he was carried on a pallet. At each assembly he would be asked to speak. And he would reply with the words, "Beloved, let us love one another." When people in the assembly listened, John spoke about love. It's so normal for him to advance to the topic of loving from the topic of listening. Wouldn't it be great if every Christian listened to every sermon and lesson partly for the purpose of maturing his loving into more of God's kind of loving? Many church feuds would have never been thought about, let alone carried through, had this been the case.

Let us love is from one word in the Greek (*agapomen*). So the first two words in this verse were built from the same word *agape*. **Beloved** (*agapetoi*) and **let us love** (*agapomen*). The idea is that we should love because we have been loved. The words **let us** are really too weak. The verb is a hortatory verb which is a command. It would be more correct to say "Beloved, we *must* love one another." This isn't an option; it's an obligation which we will clearly see stated in verse eleven.

While earlier John wrote about loving a brother (2:10), in this verse he introduced the reciprocative dimension of Christian love. Christians are to love **one another.** No Christian has the right to expect to just be loved by the other brothers or sisters. He must also love them. But why? John introduced the most powerful cause possible in this verse, **for** (which is really the word "because" [*hoti*], **love is from God.** The word **from** is *ex* from which we get our word exit. Love literally exits from God. God is where love began. No wonder the command to love goes back to the beginning (2:7), because love finds its origin in the eternal God who acted in the beginning (Gen. 1:1).

If love exits from God and if Christians are united to God, then love must flow through Christians. In fact, the love of Christians is one evidence that they are united to God — **and everyone who loves is born of God and knows God.** Does that mean that the *only* evidence of new birth is love? Not at all. Love can be counterfeited. But a continuous habit pattern of *agape*-love cannot be counterfeited. That's why John didn't say that the one who can love from time to time is born of God, but the one who loves (present tense). Love is his life-style, which is an evidence of new birth. **Is born of God** is in the perfect tense which stresses the ongoing *result* of the new birth. That ongoing result is habitual love. Not only is such a person loving, but he also **knows God** (present tense).

Notice the interrelationships between loving others, being born of God, and knowing God. There is a functional relationship between knowing God and loving others. Love is not just a feeling that we can express in any way we want to. Love doesn't come from our feelings, but from our knowings. It comes from knowing God. It involves a proper conduct because it comes from a proper content. A person who doesn't want to know more about God will not grow in his love. A person who doesn't know God at all isn't really loving, even though the outer actions may look like it. The more we know about God, the more we see His love in action and understand the character, width, depth, and breadth of it. Paul wrote about the significance of love and knowledge when he wrote, "And this I pray, that your love may abound still more and more in real knowledge and all discernment" (Phil. 1:9).

However, knowing God isn't just an intellectual knowledge. It is also an experiential knowledge that involves unity with God. That's why we read in this section about God abiding in us and we in Him (v. 13). He abides in us through the Holy Spirit (3:24); thus really knowing God involves intimate union with Him. (It is interesting to note that this word "know" was used also to describe the intimate union of a husband and wife.)

The one who does not love does not have union with God. Regardless of his claim, **he does not know God.** A person cannot claim union with God and fail to demonstrate the nature of God, **for God is love.** That's as unnatural as a person who claims to know English, but can't speak it, write it, or understand it. If he knows English, then the nature of English flows through him. And so it is with the one who knows God.

Notice that John did not say that "love is God." We come close to worshipping love as our god. We sing songs about it as if that's all the world needs — "What the world needs now is love, sweet love." Sorry, but that's not true. What the world needs now is *God*. Accept God, and love will follow. Some have deified love also by saying, "Love, then do whatever you want." Wrong again! Correct love needs correct content. John is not embarrassed by putting love and commandments in the same sentence. And neither should we be. A Christian who really wants to love also wants to know just what God's kind of love does and does not do to a person. Most of Paul's epistles were written to straighten out false notions people had about what constituted love. We don't "love and do what we want." Instead we "love and do what God wants," for **God is love** and everything He wants is an expression of love. His finest expression of love was the sending of Jesus.

II. *The Character of God's Love,* vv. 9-10

By this the love of God was manifested in us, that God has sent His only begotten Son into the world so that we might live through Him. In this is love, not that we loved God, but that He loved us and sent His Son to be the propitiation for our sins (4:9-10).

While verses 7 and 8 spotlighted one nature of God as love, this verse demonstrated several facets of the character of God's love. Consequently, if any one wants to evaluate whether or not his love is really God's kind of love, he can check it against God's love seen in these two verses.

1. *His love is expressed* — **By this the love of God was manifested.** The word **manifested** means to openly exhibit. It was used to describe the *shining* of the sun. God doesn't keep His love hidden. He makes it visible. And so should we. Love is never something we have and keep hidden.

2. *Love is other-oriented.* However, we are not to love in order to draw attention to ourselves. The sun shines in such a way that our eyes are not attracted to it, yet our lives are benefited by it. That's the way love is. Even God's love doesn't draw attention to Himself but to someone else. God drew attention to Jesus, and Jesus drew attention to God.

3. *Love holds nothing back.* God sent **his only begotten Son.** God wasn't conservative with His love. He was liberal with it. There are many examples of love in the world, but the best historical example was done when God sent Jesus. The words **only begotten** (*monogene*) literally mean "one of a kind," (*mono*-one, *gene*-kind). The word emphasizes the uniqueness of Jesus. Real love sacrifices the best for another. Do we do that? Who gets the best room and bed when guests come to your house? Do you consider what you have that is the rarest and give that away to help another?

4. *Love takes chances.* God didn't send Jesus into a protected monastery. He sent Jesus **into the world.** He sent Him directly to the front lines with all the heavy artillery firing away at full blast. And He even allowed Jesus to empty Himself and put on humanity (Phil. 2:5-11). Love takes risks. One of the needs of the church today is to become more vulnerable as she moves to meet people's needs. We need to

move more from the sanctuary to the streets, from the stained glass windows to the soiled people. It is possible to have so much going on at the church building that people have little time to be sent **into the world** with a sense of mission.

5. *Love has goals for the other person in mind.* It's one thing to be other-oriented, but it's a step beyond that to help others reach goals that benefit them. But that's why God sent Jesus — **so that we might live through Him.** God was already eternal. He didn't do this to advance His personal status. How interested are we that others catch up with us — and even pass us? Too much goes on that purposely holds people back. Our stress on competition makes us a bit jittery if someone is catching up. But God wants us to become like Him. Real love is seen when we rejoice at the other person's success.

6. *Love takes the initiative.* God didn't wait for us to make the first move — **not that we loved God, but that He loved us.** Do we wait for others to act first?

7. *Love forgives sins.* God expressed His love for perverted, polluted, and promiscuous people. That's why His love involved sending Jesus **to be the propitiation for our sins.** (See 2:2 for a discussion of this.) It is one thing to love those who are most like us; it is another thing to love those who are most *un*like us. That's what God did. And that's what love is.

When we stack up our love against these characteristics, we all probably have a lot of growing up to do. And what we have just read barely touches the hem of the garment of God's love. His love is like a diamond. No matter how you turn it, a different facet of it sparkles. Oh, for the love that manifests these many beautiful qualities.

Five times in this section John used these words, **in this** or "By this" (*en touto*). Those words stress the concept that there is *evidence* that supports the facts. This formula for stressing evidence (*en touto*) is important for John. Here are the places he used that formula with the facts he emphasized and the evidence that proves those facts:

EN TOUTO
in (or by) this

The fact	Based on evidence of
2:3 - we know him	Keeping His commandments
3:10 - children fo God	Practices righteousness and loves his brother
children of devil	Does not practice righteousness nor love his brother

3:16 - we know love	Jesus laid down His life for us
4:2 - we know the Spirit of God	Its confession of Jesus
4:9 - love of God shown	He sent His Son
4:10 - love of God	He loved us
4:13 - unity with God	He gave us His Spirit
4:17 - love is perfected	Confidence in judgment
5:2 - we are God's children	Observing God's commandments.

The point of repeating this formula so many times (*in this, by this - en touto*) is that Christianity is based on concrete support and evidences, not just on sentimentalism and emotionalism (although those are not removed from Christianity). Proper evidences direct our emotions. Emotions are not to erase evidences. God's evidences can both elevate depression and deflate superficial ecstasies. We too need to be able to say *in this* . . . is why I so live, believe, or feel.

III. *Our Obligation With God's Love*, vv. 11, 12

   A. *The Responsibility*, v. 11

   Beloved, if God so loved us, we also ought to love one another (4:11).

What God has done for us has put us in debt. We owe it to God to love others as He has loved us. The word **ought** (*opheilo*) stresses the I.O.U. aspect in Christianity. God grants His blessings *to* us so that He may **advance** His blessings *through* us to others. A Christian is to be like a river which is open on both ends — with an intake and an outflow. To take in and not give out is to become like the Dead Sea.

Some people have a difficult time with the "oughtness" of Christianity because it sounds like salvation by works. But man's functional indebtedness is also a part of God's grace. God knows how man is made, because He created us. He knows that we need to give our lives away in service to others. Psychologists are now agreeing that man needs to be needed.

God gave us responsibilities. And as we fulfill them, we become more integrated and happy as a person. That's why Paul referred to the tasks to which God called him as the grace of God, "of which I was made a minister according to the gift of God's grace . . ." (Eph. 3:7).

Two other times John used this word for debt and each time it involved imitating Jesus or God:

   The one who says he abides in Him *ought* himself to walk in the same manner as He walked (2:6).

   We know love by this, that He laid down His life for us; and we *ought* to lay down our lives for the brethren (3:16).

B. *The Result,* v. 12

No one has beheld God at any time; if we love one another, God abides in us, and His love is perfected in us (4:12).

In one sense this is one of the most powerful verses in apostolic writing. It's a parallel to John 1:18, which has two parts that I'll call Part A and Part B.

	John 1:18	I John 4:12
Part A.	No man has seen God at any time	No one has beheld God at any time
Part B.	The only begotten God who is in the bosom of the Father, He has explained Him	If we love one another, God abides in us, and His love is perfected in us.

Part A stresses the invisibility of God. God is Spirit, (John 4:24) and who can see a spirit? Although God cannot be seen, He can be known. The effects of Him can be clearly and objectively experienced. A person cannot see gravitation, but gravitation can be known and experienced. A person cannot see electricity, but electricity can be known and experienced. A person cannot see a virus, but a virus can be known and experienced. How can the invisible God be known and experienced? There are two ways which far outstrip any other way. That's what Part B in John 1:18 and I John 4:12 communicate. Jesus came to explain God. That word "explain" (*exegeomai*) literally means to bring out. The idea is that Jesus "brought out" what there was about God that could be known and laid out before us. How? By living it out. Consequently, people who wanted to see what God was like could look at Jesus—the personal model of God.

But Jesus is no longer here in person. So what do people do today when they want to see what God is like? They look at Christians. God's nature becomes visible as it flows through the lives of Christians. What Jesus did through His first century body—make God known—He wants to continue to do through His twentieth century body—the church (Eph. 1:22-23). The church is to be the on-going personal model of God's likeness.

Consequently, one result of Christians loving one another is that we make visible the effects of the invisible God. Can we carry on what Jesus began? Yes, because Jesus lives in us through the Spirit (John 14:18, 19). Indeed **God abides in us.** And when we love others with His kind of love, **His love is perfected in us.** The word **perfected** (*teleioo*) means brought to its intended usage. God's intended purpose of our fulfilling our I.O.U. to love others is that they, too, can know God. People simply will not relate to God's love in the sending of His unique Son (v. 9, 10), if they do not experience His love in the present through His many sons and daughters—His personal model.

How are we doing in giving people a real life audio-visual aid of God's nature? Here is a biblical motivation for an incarnational missionary work — that is to put flesh and bones to our witness. This personal witness has something to say against reducing our outreach to only the electronic church. People need the experience of being *with* people in whom God lives to "see" a demonstration of God's life. They will not get that needed dimension through television and radio alone. Our emphasis on electronic evangelism and edification may make stars out of certain personalities, but it may also make the image of God too remote. No Christian can fellowship with transistors. Too many electronic preachers are getting people more hooked to a channel than to a church. We are not to be connected to electricity but to the *ekklesia,* the assembly of God's people who are to model Him.

IV. *Some Certainties in Love,* vv. 13-18
   A. *Our Present Consolation,* vv. 13-16

By this we know that we abide in Him and He in us, because He has given us of His Spirit. And we have beheld and bear witness that the Father has sent the Son to be the Savior of the world. Whoever confesses that Jesus is the Son of God, God abides in him, and he in God. And we have come to know and have believed the love which God had for us. God is love, and the one who abides in love abides in God, and God abides in him (4:13-16).

While love is the functional *manifestation* that God abides in us (v. 12), the Holy Spirit is the *means* by which God abides in us. When the Holy Spirit dwells in us, God dwells in us (Eph. 2:22). That's why John said, **By this we know that we abide in Him and He in us, because He has given us of His Spirit.**

However, the Spirit is not given in isolation from the activity of the **Father** and the **Son. The Father has sent,** and so the Son became the **Savior of the world.** His death for us made it possible for us to be united with God through the Spirit. It is through Jesus that we "have our access in one Spirit to the Father" (Eph. 2:18). His death became the means for our forgiveness, and our forgiveness cleansed us for the indwelling of God's Spirit. But all that God has done for our consolation with Him must be met with our confession of Jesus (v. 15).

Consequently, the historical facts of the activity of the Father (who sent), the Son (who came), the Holy Spirit (who indwells), and the Christians (who confess) give objective evidence to unity. That unity is two dimensional: (1) a unity with deity—God, (2) a unity with humanity—God's children, (Eph. 2:18-19). The evidence of the two dimensional unity must be expressed in the realm of both dimensions — a love to God and a love to God's children. To love only one of those dimensions gives evidence that the unity is counterfeit (I John 4:20).

   B. *Our Future Confidence,* v. 17, 18

   By this, love is perfected with us, that we may have confidence in the day of judgment; because as He is, so also are we in this world. There is no fear in love; but perfect love casts out fear, because fear involves punishment, and the one who fears is not perfected in love (4:17, 18).

Not only does our love express present unity with both God and God's children, but it also gives us confidence that the unity will not cease after the day of judgment. God's love in us is brought to its intended usage (**perfected**—See verse 12) not only during this life as we love others, but at the end of this life **in the day of judgment.**

This day is called not only the day of judgment but also the last day (John 6:39), the great day (Rev. 6:17), the day of God (Rev. 16:14). On that day the entire world will be judged (Matt. 25:31-43). Those who are not united to God will be terror stricken, regardless of their earthly status (Rev. 6:12-17). While the haters will run *from* God with cowardice, the lovers in Christ will run *to* God with confidence.

The confidence is not pride in self but boldness in the Savior. Why shouldn't the Christian be confident if He trusts God? God will keep His promises. He is trustworthy. The Christian does not have to wait until that day to know whether or not he is saved. Is God living in Him as seen by God's love living through Him? If so, then the Christian is living in the world as Jesus is — **as He is, so also are we in this world.** No wonder we can have confidence. Jesus was not condemned, and neither is the Christian (Rom. 8:1). If we are united with Christ, we are united with the conqueror, because He destroyed the works of the Devil. And we enter into His victory.

So loving as He loved, which is **perfect love,** casts out fear. With the practice of love is the presence of confidence. And with the presence of confidence is the absence of fear. This doesn't mean we do not respect God, but it does mean that we do not retreat from Him in the anticipation of punishment. We often fear whom we do not love. And we often do not love whom we do not know. Children are often afraid of strangers. But friendship and the love that grow out of it erase the fear. The child who fears a person who loves him does it for only one reason — his love hasn't matured as it should have. Perhaps his familiarity with the person has been too skimpy to properly mature his love. The more isolated we remain from God, the more *under*developed will be our love and the more *over*developed will be our fear. That's just nature. I am always

CHAPTERS 4, 5   I JOHN 4:7 – 5:5

somewhat intimidated in the presence of important people. But the more I know them, the more I love them and the less I fear them. So it is between us and God.

V. *The Sharing of God's Love*, v. 19

We love, because He first loved us (4:19).

Instead of living in fear (v. 18), the Christian lives in love. But we did not initiate love. God did. We merely share what He first did. **We love** Him and others **because He first loved us.** Love has a way of multiplying itself. Love is in the cloning business. Each of us should become clones of God's love. The only reason we can love at all with *agape*-love is because that is the nature of God in whose image we were first created and then recreated (Gen. 1:27; Eph. 4:24). He first loved and then invited us to be a partaker of His divine nature (II Pet. 1:4).

VI. *The Integrity of Love*, vv. 20, 21

    A. *With Our Confession*, v. 20

If some one says, "I love God," and hates his brother, he is a liar; for the one who does not love his brother whom he has seen cannot love God whom he has not seen (4:20).

With whom are we to express love? To both God and God's children. In fact, we prove to the Father that we love Him by loving all those whom He has begotten. The capacity to love God is at the same time the capacity to love our Christian brother. If we are not (present tense) loving our brothers, we prove that we do not have the capacity to love God. That's another way of saying that the failure to love the brothers is to functionally acknowledge that God does not live in us. For when God lives in us, love does also. The confession "I love God" is backed up by the conduct of loving the brothers. The sentence from the lips must be shown from the love.

    B. *With God's Commandment*, v. 21

And this commandment we have from Him, that the one who loves God should love his brother also (4:21).

A person who will not obey God cannot love God. And the person does not obey God if he is not obeying his most inclusive command—love. Love for both God and others is such a single aspect that it is referred to here as *one* commandment. Love is the supreme command. It tests whether or not we have properly obeyed the other commands.

Have we really believed, repented, confessed, and been immersed into Jesus? Our love life can tell us.

While love is the supreme command, it is never to be seen as the "lone-ranger" aspect in Christianity. Some people have so stressed the concept of love that they have telescoped all of Christianity into this one four-lettered word. Love must be correctly integrated with other essentials in Christianity, which was John's next emphasis.

VII. *The Integration of Love,* 5:1-5

Whoever believes that Jesus is the Christ is born of God; and whoever loves the Father loves the child born of Him. By this we know that we love the children of God, when we love God and observe His commandments. For this is the love of God, that we keep His commandments; and His commandments are not burdensome. For whatever is born of God overcomes the world: and this is the victory that has overcome the world — our faith. And who is the one who overcomes the world, but he who believes that Jesus is the Son of God? (5:1-5).

In this section, we see the integrated relationship of most of what John had been discussing. Jesus, belief, birth, God's family, commandments, obedience, love of God, love of children, and victory are related and cross-related. Notice how many times some of these concepts were used within these five verses: belief (1, 4, 5), love (1, 2, 3), obey (2, 3), Jesus (1, 5). The section began and ended with Jesus (1, 5). And why not? He is both the Alpha and the Omega — the first and the last (Rev. 1:12). He is both the author and perfector of our faith (Heb. 12:2).

It is possible to see this relationship in the following circle:

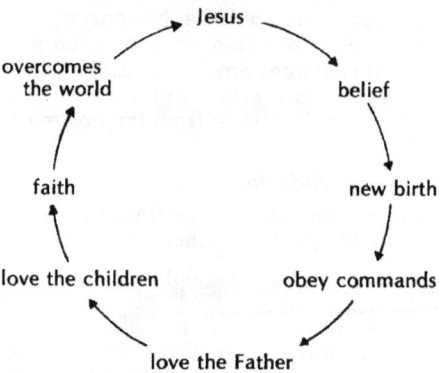

New birth (**is born** — perfect tense which stresses abiding results) is evidenced by the fact that the person continues to believe in Jesus (present tense) and continues to love the Father and His children (v. 1). Notice that our belief in Jesus and behavior toward Christians are related. They cannot be divorced. They are twin evidences of our position.

However, love is not just a feeling. It is concrete, not abstract. We know we are loving (present tense) when we are observing (present tense) God's commandments (v. 2). Those two activities (observing commandments and loving) are co-related. That's because all of God's commandments come wrapped in the package of love. He has never commanded anything that is not for our benefit.

That's why **his commandments are not burdensome** (v. 3). The word for **burdensome** (*bareo*) refers to something so heavy that it weighs down a person or breaks him down. God's commands will not break us down.

Jesus said it in a positive way, "For My yoke is easy, and My load is light" (Matthew 11:30). The word "easy" means well-fitted. There is a tradition that Jesus kept a sign over His work bench at the carpenter's shop that read, "My yokes are easy." Jesus would never make a yoke for a team of oxen until He first looked at the team, handled them, and measured them. Then He would tailor-make His yokes so they would fit so well that the load the oxen pulled would become lighter due to the fit of the yoke. His yoke caused no friction on the shoulders of those oxen.

God's commands are like that. He knows us because He made us. His commands are tailor-made for our shoulders. They do not get heavy, for they square with our new inner nature.

Even the world cannot weigh us down, **for whatever is born of God overcomes the world.** The words **is born** is again the perfect tense which stresses abiding results. Another present result of our past new birth is that we are making it a habit pattern to overcome the world (v. 4). While our belief affects our behavior with others (v. 1), it also affects our behavior with the world (v. 4). And why not? For to love God and His children is to not love the world; and the person who doesn't love the world will not be taken captive by it.

The activity of overcoming and believing are co-related (v. 5), as are the activities of loving and obeying (v. 2), and all of these are cross-related. Believing leads to loving; loving leads to obeying. Obeying directs loving. Obeying leads to overcoming. One of the things of the world that is overcome is hatred which frees a person to love more, and on and on the cycle goes.

This entire section of "life in the Spirit" began by testing a person's confession of Jesus (4:2) and ends at that same place (5:5). If the one who believes in Jesus is overcoming the world, then the one who isn't believing is being overcome by the world. Now we see one of the goals of the spirit of the antichrist (4:3). The antichrists want to overcome us, but we must never give in. Keep believing; keep loving; keep obeying — and you will keep overcoming.

THIRTEEN LESSONS ON I, II AND III JOHN

QUESTIONS FOR DISCUSSION:
1. What is the relationship of 4:7-12 with 4:3?
2. In light of verses 7-15, what are the criteria for having confidence in the day of judgment?
3. List ways to be in the world "as He is in the world" (v. 17).
4. What does question 3 have to do with being the "body of Christ"?
5. How does the Holy Spirit give us evidence that God is in us and we are in God?
6. Why do we love? Whom do we love? How do we love? When do we love?
7. What is "perfect love"?
8. What does believing have to do with loving?
9. Why do people think that God's commandments are burdensome?

Part Six

LIFE IN ASSURANCE

The antichrists will try to weaken us at the first stage of Christianity — belief. They will sow seeds of doubt in our minds. But we can live in assurance not doubt. John turned to that thought as his final exhortation to his readers who were being bombarded with the seeds of doubt.

Lesson Eleven
(5:6-21)

LIFE IN ASSURANCE

I. Our Assurance in the Historicity of Jesus, vv. 6-10
   A. The Historical Evidence, v. 6
   B. The Holy Spirit's Evidence, v. 7
   C. The Combined Evidence, vv. 8-9
   D. The Subjective Evidence, v. 10

II. Our Assurance in Salvation, vv. 11-13
   A. God's Promise for Us, vv. 11-12
   B. God's Publication to Us, v. 13

III. Our Assurance in Prayer, vv. 14-17
   A. A Condition for Prayer, v. 14
   B. A Confidence in Prayer, v. 15
   C. A Charge for Prayer, vv. 16-17

IV. Our Assurance for Living in This World, vv. 18-21
   A. Our Sonship, vv. 18-19
   B. Jesus' Sonship, v. 20
   C. Our Surveillance, v. 21

Being an overcomer is a popular topic today. Everybody wants to be a winner. But Jesus Christ has already won (v. 5). Consequently, anyone in Him simultaneously stands in the victory lane. So when everything nailed down seems to be coming up, the Christian can stand assured that he has made the right choice of priorities. To those whose confidence was being attacked by the philosophers and the politicians, John concluded his communication with a repeated emphasis upon assurance.

I. *Our Assurance in the Historicity of Jesus,* vv. 6-10
   A. *The Historical Evidence,* v. 6

   This is the one who came by water and blood, Jesus Christ; not with the water only, but with the water and with the blood (5:6).

   John had just stated that Jesus had overcome the world (v. 5). But was it a real Jesus, an imagined Jesus, or a symbolic Jesus? It was the *real* Jesus who lived in the midst of *real* history. The historical evidence of His objective reality abounds. **This is the one** picks up the similar phrase "who is the one?" (*estin ho*) in verse five. The victorious one in verse five is the historical one in verse six. The one who overcame the world is the one who came to the world. "The Son of God" in verse five is **Jesus Christ** in verse six. And His coming can be historically checked out, for he **came by water and blood.** Literally, the Greek says He came *through* water and blood. Water and blood were not the *means* of His coming but the *manner* in which He came. But to what does **water and blood** refer? There have been several suggestions:

   1. Purification and redemption, which would stress Jesus' function. In the Old Testament water can refer to purification (Lev. 14:52), and blood can refer to redemption (Heb. 9:19).
   2. Baptism and the Lord's Supper in the church, which stress the ritualistic aspect.
   3. Jesus' baptism and the cross, which stress the historical aspect.

   The best understanding of **water and blood** is baptism and the cross. Connected to those two historical events are the other two explanations — purification/redemption and baptism/the Lord's Supper in the church.

   But what does Jesus' baptism and the cross have in common so that together they stressed the manner of Jesus' historical coming? They have much in common. Here is a partial list:

   1. Both stress Jesus' humility.
   2. Both stress Jesus' identification with humans.
   3. Both picture a death scene.
   4. Both precede a resurrection.

5. Both were witnessed by a multitude of people. Their historicity stands on historical evidence.
6. Both received the testimony of God. At the baptism, God spoke through words. At the cross, God spoke through nature in the earthquake and darkness.
7. Baptism is referred to as a death (Rom. 6), and the cross is referred to as a baptism (Mark 10:39).
8. Both are connected to Jesus' public ministry. Through baptism, He entered the public ministry. Through the cross and resurrection He finished His public ministry. His apostles were to be followers of Jesus from those two focal points (Acts 2:22).
9. Jesus' disciples today are to follow Him in submitting to baptism (Matt. 28:19, 20; Acts 2:38) and in taking up a cross (Matt. 10:38). Both are a self-denial which are to be done in history as were Jesus' acts of self-denial done in history.
10. Both spoke directly to the philosophical heresy which was being used to undermine the confidence of Christians in John's day. One group (Docetics) said that Jesus was just a phantom. But a phantom cannot be immersed in front of a crowd of witnesses nor be nailed to the cross with a flow of blood evident for all to see.

    Another group (Cerinthics) claimed that Jesus was not divine until the Spirit came to Him at His baptism, and He was not divine on the cross because the Holy Spirit left Him while He was in the garden. So Jesus wasn't divine *before* baptism nor *on* the cross. John denied both of those by saying that Jesus (the *human* aspect) and Christ (the *divine* aspect) came *through* both the baptism and the cross. He was both human and divine on both sides of (*through*) both events.

To further defuse those who claimed that Jesus was divine at His baptism but not on the cross, John wrote **not with water only but with the water and with the blood.** The word with (*en*) literally means "in." He was divine not only prior to and after each event but also while He was "in" the midst of each event. How was Jesus' divinity demonstrated prior to and after each of those events? The following chart will demonstrate it:

JESUS' DIVINITY SHOWN

Before	After
Baptism - Virgin conception	Miracles/total life
The cross - Miracles/total life	Post-resurrection appearances and the sending of the Spirit.

CHAPTER 5   I JOHN 5:6-21

It would be difficult to explain the culmination of baptism and the Lord's Supper over a twentieth century span without the historical anchor of the water and the blood in Jesus' earth-walk.

Not only was the divinity of Jesus present then, but His super-natural presence and power are also with us now while we are in the midst of those two events in our lives. That was a shattering statement to the philosophical pagans, but it reassured the Christians.

  B. *The Holy Spirit's Evidence,* v. 7

And it is the Spirit who bears witness, because the Spirit is the truth (5:7).

Not only is human history a witness to the fact that Jesus Christ is the Son of God, but God's Spirit is also a witness to that fact. While history is something done in the past, the Spirit's witness is not restricted to one time zone. He bore witness in the past and still **bears witness** (present tense). The Spirit bore witness in the past by confirming Jesus' earthly life with signs and wonders (Acts 2:22), coming to Jesus at His baptism, confirming the witness of His apostles (Acts 2:43; 14:1, 2; Heb. 2:1-4), and inspiring His apostles and prophets (I Cor. 2). He continues to bear witness through the written Word (Eph. 6:17), by convicting men (John 16:8), by dwelling within men (I Cor. 6:19, 20), by sealing men (Eph. 1:13, 14), and by uniting men to God and to each other (Eph. 2:17-22; 4:3).

The Spirit's primary function is to testify about Jesus *to us, in us,* and *through us* (John 15:26; 16:14). **The Spirit is the truth** because He will not speak on His own initiative, but whatever He hears He will speak (John 16:13). The Spirit is the mouthpiece of God. And God does not lie. No wonder the Spirit is the truth.

Today, the sword of the Spirit is the Word of God (Eph. 6:17). If we want to stand on truth we must stand on the Word of God. To neglect the Word for subjective feelings is a trap laid by the devil.

  C. *The Combined Evidence,* vv. 8, 9

For there are three that bear witness, the Spirit and the water and the blood: and the three are in agreement. If we receive the witness of men, the witness of God is greater; for the witness of God is this, that He has borne witness concerning His Son (5:8, 9).

There is strength in numbers and particularly so when it comes to witnesses. In the Old Testament two or three witnesses firmly established facts (Deut. 17:6; 19:15). Just try to get three people to agree on every minute detail of any historical happening. That's super hard. There isn't one minor detail of Jesus' life that is contradicted by the testimony of the water, blood and Spirit. The Spirit even inspired the prophecy of minor details of Jesus' life and those were fulfilled. Most of them were fulfilled between the water and the blood which covered the span of Jesus' ministry. No wonder John wrote **and the three are in agreement** which literally said, "and the three are into the one" (*kai hoi treis eis to hen eisin*). The three are so consistent that their witness merges into just one—that Jesus Christ is the Son of God.

The concept of *oneness* has often been used as evidence of *one God* (Eph. 4:4-6). Paul made the point that God is the God of all people—Jews and Gentiles—because He is one (Rom. 3:29, 30). The one God produces one people (Gal. 3:29). So it's not unusual for the God to have *three* witnesses that "are into the one."

These three kinds of witnesses were in identical agreement because they were really **the witness of God.** When God sits on the witness stand, the jury would do well to play back the transcript and let His testimony be the verdict without any debate. **The witness of God is greater** than the witness of man because it agrees at every point about the most important historical event—Jesus.

John reaffirmed confidence in his readers by calling these divine witnesses to the stand. John is very concerned about historical evidence of the Christ-event. In his Gospel he listed seven different witnesses to Jesus.

    1. John the Baptist, 1:7
    2. Christ's works, 5:3
    3. The Father, 5:37
    4. Scripture, 5:39-47
    5. Christ's words, 8:14, 18
    6. The Spirit, 15:26
    7. The disciples, 15:27

For a good resource in further evidences for Christianity see *New Testament Evidences* by Wallace Wartick (College Press) and *Evidence That Demands A Verdict* by Josh McDowell (Campus Crusade).

 D. *The Subjective Evidence,* v. 10

> **The one who believes in the Son of God has the witness in himself; the one who does not believe God has made him a liar, because he has not believed in the witness that God has borne concerning His Son (5:10).**

While verses 6-9 stressed the objective evidence, this verse stressed the subjective evidence. God didn't place all the evidence for Jesus outside of us. He put significant evidence inside of us, but there is a condition for that inner witness— **the one who believes in the Son of God has the witness in himself.** Literally the Greek says, "the one who is believing *into* (*eis*) the Son . . ." There is a difference between believing *in* (*en*) and believing *into* (*eis*). To believe *into* stresses a movement from outside whatever you believe to inside of it. In other words, the belief has moved the person to an identification with whatever he trusts. Thirty-four times in his Gospel, John used this same formula—believe into (*pisteuo eis*).

When our belief moves us into Jesus in such a way that Jesus is in us and we are in Jesus, then we have **the witness** in ourselves. What is that inner witness? It is the Holy Spirit (I John 3:24). Paul said it this way, "The Spirit Himself bears witness with our spirit that we are children of God" (Rom. 8:16). Some people are so uncomfortable with the idea of the Holy Spirit that they restrict the Holy Spirit to only the written Word. But the written Word is *not* the Holy Spirit. A person cannot purchase the "Holy Spirit" at K-Mart for five dollars. The Bible is the product of the Spirit and the sword of the Spirit, but is not the Spirit. The Spirit dwells in people (Rom. 8:11). God has "sent forth the Spirit of His Son into our hearts . . ." (Gal. 4:6).

The presence of the Spirit is our subjective evidence that Jesus is God's Son and that we are God's children through Jesus. However, a person cannot equate the presence of the Spirit to some kind of tingling inner feeling. The Spirit's presence rests upon objective evidence of Jesus and objective commands of God for receiving the Spirit (Acts 2:38; 5:32). The subjective witness we claim must never be used to by-pass the objective Word God commanded. Nor must we reduce our confidence in whether or not we have the Spirit to whether or not we *feel* like we have Him. God made a promise to us (Acts 2:38, 39), and He keeps His promises. It is by His promises that we have become partakers of the divine nature (II Peter 1:5). Thus if we fulfilled what He asked, we should claim the presence of the Holy Spirit with confidence. Feeling has nothing to do with it. But the declaration of God has everything to do with it. We must trust His declaration and not our feelings. I never felt married the second after the wedding ceremony, but I was married. So it is with having the witness of the Spirit in us.

II. *Our Assurance in Salvation,* vv. 11-13

   A. *God's Promise for Us,* vv. 11, 12

And the witness is this, that God has given us eternal life, and this life is in His Son. He who has the Son has the life; he who does not have the Son of God does not have eternal life (5:11, 12).

God's witness doesn't stop at just who Jesus is, but also includes what is ours because of Jesus. These verses underscore several significant truths:

1. **Life** is in the Son (See also John 5:26).
2. Eternal life for us is a gift—**has given.**

3. Only **God** can give it.
4. The gift is given conditionally — **he who has the Son has the life.**
5. The gift was given in the past with abiding results — **has given** (perfect tense). Thus we should demonstrate the fruit of it.
6. The gift is not just a past event but also a present reality — **has the life.**
7. The life is a *quality* life — **eternal** stresses kind as well as time.
8. The life is also a quantative life — a new kind of clock — forever.
9. The Christian can know that he is saved.
10. The non-Christian is not saved.

B. *God's Publication to Us,* v. 13

These things I have written to you who believe in the name of the Son of God, in order that you may know that you have eternal life (5:13).

It's somewhat of a tragedy that many Christians live their earthly life wondering whether or not they are saved. Many look as if they are attending an eternal funeral. We are not to live our lives as if we are facing a final exam for which we are not prepared.

John wants Christians to **know that you have eternal life.** That's why he wrote what he wrote. If we do not know whether or not we are saved, we don't trust the Bible. In fact, we don't even trust God, for God has taken the witness stand and declared, "He who has the Son has the life" (v. 12). Are we going to sit in the jury box and veto His witness? John doesn't want us living out our Christianity as if we are attending an ongoing T.V. quiz show in which the correct answer won't be revealed until the end. John has made it as clear as possible. **These things I have written to you who believe in the name of the Son of God, in order that you may know that you have eternal life.** That settles it! Believe it and live it. In Christ there is no condemnation (Rom. 8:1). *In* Him there is no fear about the judgment day when we will appear before Him (2:28; 4:17, 18). In Him we have eternal life.

One reason God published His promises was to assure us of what is ours — now. If someone asks you, "Are you saved?" Answer "yes" or "no." John eliminated the twilight zone of assurance, because God eliminated it in Jesus Christ.

This is the last time John used the word "believe," but nine times in this short writing he discussed the Christian's belief. However, John did not write meaningless repetition. As he did with the topic of love, John's teaching about belief accelerated somewhat with each mention of it. (See the chart on the following page.)

CHAPTER 5

I JOHN 5:6-21

JOHN'S ACCELERATED TEACHING ABOUT BELIEF

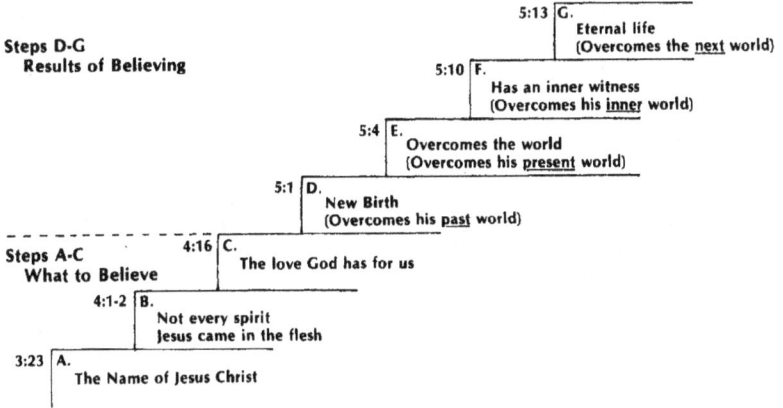

III. *Our Assurance in Prayer, vv. 14-17*
   A. *A Condition for Prayer, v. 14*

   And this is the confidence which we have before Him, that, if we ask anything according to His will, He hears us (5:14).

This is the fourth time John used the word confidence (*parresia*) in this writing. Twice, confidence referred to the judgment (2:28; 4:17) and twice to prayer (3:21; 5:14). While one dealt with what we expect to hear from God in the future (judgment), the other dealt with what God hears from us in the present (prayer).

To say we have confidence **before Him** really stresses the idea that we are in His presence. The word for **before** is the same word John used to describe the presence of Jesus with God (John 1:1 — translated here "with God" — *pros*).

Anytime the Christian is in the presence of God, whether *there* or *here*, he can have confidence (or experience freedom, for that's what the Greek word for confidence stresses). The Christian will not be tied up in knots when he is in the presence of God. God's presence does not threaten us as does the presence of some important humans. God is too humble, too serving, too loving, too compassionate, too outgoing to let that happen to us. Nothing is more natural than for the child to be in the presence of his Father. No one would be more "at ease" in the presence of the President of the United States than his children. They do not fear their father's presidential judgments, and they experience complete freedom to talk with Him. They can ask the President to tie their shoes or to give them a hug. What a freedom! But the Christian has more freedom than that with the Creator (Phil. 4:6).

Confidence in prayer rests upon us asking **according to His will.** This doesn't mean that every specific request must square with what God has already decided. God doesn't decide ahead of time which shirt He wants us to buy or which car to drive. He gives us freedom to make those choices. He is big enough to bless us in a wide range of choices. He is Lord of the entire universe and offers us the beauty of variety.

But this condition for prayer does mean that our specific requests should square with God's general will — that is, we use our life and possessions to further enhance His desire for all humans on planet earth. (See *How To Know The Will Of God;* Standard Publishing). If our request interferes with God's universal purpose, He will not listen to it (James 4:1-3). He will not let either our prayers or our practices eliminate His plans. **According to His will** cannot be divorced from "keeping His commandments" (3:22).

B. *A Confidence in Prayer,* v. 15

And if we know that He hears us in whatever we ask, we know that we have the requests which we have asked from Him (5:15).

We know He hears us when we ask according to His will. And when that happens we know that **we have the requests** we have asked. The word **have** is in the present tense. The idea is that when we ask according to God's will, we *already* have the answer even though the specific details or the package in which the answer resides have not yet arrived. God says "yes" as we pray, then gives us the dividends of the "yes" at the time He knows it is most needed. What a fantastic promise! When we pray **according to His will** we become partners with God in the way we pray and for what we pray (II Cor. 1:11). Just think what would happen if we prayed more?

C. *A Charge for Prayer,* vv. 16-17

If any one sees his brother committing a sin not leading to death, he shall ask and God will for him give life to those who commit sin not leading to death. There is a sin leading to death; I do not say that he should make request for this. All unrighteousness is sin, and there is a sin not leading to death (5:16, 17).

John charged his readers to intercede in prayer when **he sees his brother committing a sin.** This charge alone makes it clear that at no time in this writing did John intend to communicate that a Christian never sins (3:6, 9); otherwise this charge would be meaningless. As Jesus is interceding for us in heaven (2:1), we should intercede for one another on

CHAPTER 5　　　　　　　　　　　　　　　　　　　　　　　I JOHN 5:6-21

earth, not only by prayer but also by personal confrontation (Matt. 18:15-17), admonition (I Thess. 5:14), personal effort to detour the person from sin (Gal. 6:1; James 5:19-20), and church discipline (I Cor. 5:18; Rom. 6:17; Titus 3:10).

But what is **a sin not leading to death** and what is **a sin leading to death?** Many answers have been proposed. Some commentators say that this is the most difficult verse in the New Testament. The difficulty does not lie in only the verse itself, but also in our theological glasses that automatically blind us to certain answers. One thing is certain — John's readers clearly knew what John was talking about, which is why John did not clarify his descriptions.

Here are some of the suggestions for the sin which leads to death:

1. A deliberate sin (Lev. 4:2, 13, 22; Numbers 15:27-31). But this is unlikely because most of our sins are deliberate. Jesus prayed for people who deliberately sinned (Luke 22:32).
2. Those sins which result in capital punishment according to the laws of the land. However, Christians did pray for such people (Acts 16:16; II Cor. 1:8-11).
3. Sin which leads to physical death (Acts 5:1-11; I Cor. 11:30). But which sins are those? They can surely be prayed for, since Paul commanded the church to repent from them. The word for **life** which God will give is *not* the word for physical life (*bios*), but eternal life (*zoe*). Consequently, the death he is headed toward is not physical death. Given enough time all of us will die physically.
4. Sins which lead to excommunication from the church (I Cor. 5). Again these can surely be prayed for, since Paul wrote to help people repent from them.
5. Post-baptismal sin. All sins Christians do are post-baptismal. John records Jesus' call for people to repent of post-baptismal sins (Rev. 2, 3).
6. Blasphemy against the Holy Spirit (Mark 3:29; Matt. 12:32; Luke 12:10).
7. Total apostasy.
8. The sins John outlined in this writing that show that a person is an antichrist.

Which one of these (if any) is the candidate for the answer? Let's work up to arriving at an answer by doing some analysis of the verse and the situation.

Here are some truths we can know about this verse:

1. **A brother** in the New Testament refers to either another human or another Christian; however, John has consistently used the term

"little children" to refer to Christians. Consequently, the brother in this context refers to another Christian who is a brother because he was born of God (5:1, 18). John used the word **brother** fourteen other times in I John and each time it referred to another Christian (2:9, 10, 14; 3:10-17; 4:20-21).

2. **Sin** is lawlessness (3:4) and unrighteousness (5:17).
3. **Life** (*zoe*) is always eternal life in I John (1:1, 2; 2:25; 3:14, 15; 5:11-13, 16, 20). **Death** is then the opposite of eternal life (3:14).

It is clear that a Christian brother can sin in such a way that he is headed toward (*pros*) death — that means he is headed toward stepping outside the sphere of eternal life. While many today do not accept this possibility, the New Testament was not so reluctant (Hebrews 2:1-4; 3:7 — 4:13; 6:1-20; 10:19-39; 12:1-29; I Cor. 5; I Tim. 1:18-20; II Tim. 4:10; Rev. 2, 3; Gal. 1:8; 4:8-9; 5:1-7; 6:7-10; James 5:19-20; II Thess. 3:14; Col. 2:8; II Cor. 6:14-18; John 15:1-6).

It is possible to commit a sin that is so serious that it cuts a Christian off from eternal life. There is no reason for us to disregard the rest of I John and the situation his readers were in. John's readers were being lured to walk away from Jesus. When a person is lured by false teaching (or pressure from dictators) to disbelieve that Jesus is God's Son who came in the flesh, he is being lured **toward** eternal death. Such a person would not love the Christians and would live in sin as a habit pattern of his life. That's the style of the antichrists, some of whom had at one time been a part of the Christian community. When a person goes that far, he has committed apostasy, which is probably the state of blasphemy against the Holy Spirit. For such a person intercessory prayer is not forbidden; it is simply not commanded.

Other sins of a brother do not lead to death (v. 17). A Christian does not step into and out of the family of God every time he sins. As Christians, we are in God's family where there is security. I do not kick my children out of our human family every time they sin. And neither does God do that with us. The Christian life is an experience of progression, not of perfection. Our Father is patient, loving, and forgiving. In this entire section, John stressed our security; however, he included this one verse to remind us that apostasy is not impossible. But the Christian should not allow this possibility to dominate his thoughts. We are to live in the world with force not fear, power not paralysis, confidence not cowardice.

IV. *Our Assurance for Living in This World*, vv. 18-21
   A. *Our Sonship*, vv. 18, 19

> **We know that no one who is born of God sins; but he who was born of God keeps him and the evil one does not touch him.**

we know that we are of God, and the whole world lies in the power of the evil one (5:18, 19).

It is clear by these verses that there is security in the family of God. Our Father is in the business of keeping us (present tense). And as He does that, **the evil one does not touch us.** The word **touch** does not mean the Devil cannot tempt us or hurt us with sin. It is a word (*hapto*) which means to cling to. It's another way of saying that the Christian does not live **in the power of the evil one** as the world does (v. 19). God will not let the Devil snatch us out of His family. God will not give in to the desires of the evil one (I Cor. 10:13). However, God does continue to give us the freedom of choice. While the Devil does not have the power to grab us from God, we do have the power to walk away from our Father. If we commit apostasy, we cannot blame the devil. Apostasy is a person's own decision. That's why there is so much in the New Testament to detour us from that route. No Christian *has* to. If he does it, he *wants* to. What a tragedy to disown one's spiritual family!

B. *Jesus' Sonship*, v. 20

And we know that the Son of God has come, and has given us understanding, in order that we might know Him who is true, and we are in Him who is true, in His Son Jesus Christ. This is the true God and eternal life (5:20).

As the Christian can face the world in the assurance that he faces it as God's child in the protective care of God, he also faces the world assured that Jesus is the Son of God who **has come.** The Greek verb for has come (*hekei*) is in the present tense. However, this particular verb stresses a past coming of someone who is still present. It can be translated "is present." Jesus came in flesh in the first century and He is still present in flesh—our flesh—because He has taken up residence in us. Thus the Christian faces the world in the presence of Jesus who dwells within him.

But how did the coming of Jesus give us **understanding**? He lived out the character and purpose of God (John 1:18; 4:34) **in order that we might know Him who is true.** God is the **one who is true.** And we can be united to Him—**we are in Him who is true.** That unity with God comes only as we are **in His Son Jesus Christ.** Jesus not only provides *understanding* about God, but also *unity* with God. That was Jesus' prayer for us (John 17), and that was His achievement for us (Eph. 2).

But how can unity with Jesus be at the same time a unity with God? Because Jesus is God who came in the flesh. **This is the true God and eternal life.** This is another way to say, "In the beginning was the Word and the Word was with God, and the Word was God" (John 1:1).

No wonder the Christian can face the world with assurance. He faces the world with God who is the Creator, Lord, and Judge of the world.

THIRTEEN LESSONS ON I, II AND III JOHN

To face the world with God is to face the world with supreme power. So it is foolish to think about turning from the **true God** to idols. And that's John's last word.

This is the last time John used the word "know" in I John, but, he used it thirty-seven times throughout I John. He wanted Christians to know what they could know. The words he used (*ginosko* and *oida*) stressed certainty that is based upon experience and evidence. Christians aren't to just "suppose" and "assume," but know with assurance. Here is a list of twenty-six truths John says we can know as Christians:

1. Our advocate, 2:3, 4
2. We are in Him, 2:5
3. The Father, 2:13-14
4. It is the last hour, 2:18
5. Our anointing, 2:20
6. The truth, 2:21
7. Jesus is righteous, 2:29
8. Who is born of Him, 2:29
9. We shall be like Him, 3:2
10. Why Jesus came, 3:5
11. We have passed out of death into life, 3:14
12. A murderer does not have life, 3:15
13. Love, 3:16
14. We are of the truth, 3:19
15. He abides in us, 3:24
16. The Spirit of God, 4:2
17. The spirit of truth and error, 4:6
18. God, 4:7
19. God's love for us, 4:10
20. We abide in Him and He in us, 4:13
21. We love the children of God, 5:2
22. We have eternal life, 5:13
23. He hears us, 5:15
24. We have our requests, 5:15
25. No one who is born of God sins, 5:20
26. Jesus is the true, Divine One, 5:20

Each one of these truths is supported by knowable evidence. There are several reasons why a person may not accept the Gospel. He may not hear, may not understand, may not want to accept it but he cannot correctly insist that there is insufficient evidence for supporting the claims of the Gospel. Evidence abounds. The person can *know*.

C. *Our Surveillance*, v. 21

Little children, guard yourselves from idols (5:21).

CHAPTER 5   I JOHN 5:6-21

The Christian can be lured to throw God aside for idols. If that were not possible, John would not have written this verse. We must be on the alert so that we do not allow that to happen. It can happen if we turn to the philosophers for "truth" or deify the politicians as our "lords." Both were the immediate threats to John's readers. To do that is to deny Jesus. It can also happen if our traditions, buildings, or programs become the reason we do what we do.

To live in assurance does not mean we live in absurdity. The Devil is real. He's a master deceiver. He will try to get us to disbelieve in the human-Divine Jesus who came in historical flesh (1:1-4); he will try to convince us that sin doesn't really matter (1:5-23); he will try to get us to neglect the commands of God (2:4-6); he will try to get us to neglect our brothers (2:2-11); he will try to get us to forget our spiritual heritage (2:12-14); he will try to get us to love the world (2:15-17); he will try to get us to listen to the antichrists (2:18-29); he will try to get us to doubt the love God has for us (3:1-3); he will try to lure us into continuous sin 3:4-24); he will try to align us with false teachers (4:1-6), inadequate love (4:7 — 5:5), and doubt (5:6-20). We must not pay attention to any of it. God is true **and we are in Him who is true, in His Son Jesus Christ. This is the true God and eternal life. Little children, guard yourselves from idols.**

How can we guard ourselves from idols? By remembering and applying every truth in this small writing from John — especially those aspects he stressed repeatedly: belief (nine times), righteousness (five times), love (fifty-six times in one form or another) knowledge (thirty-seven times), and abiding (nineteen times).

The finest way to stay away from idols is by abiding in the true One. That's one reason John stressed the word "abide" (*meno*) so often. Nineteen times he used it. There is an essential relationship between those words he used repeatedly in such a short space — belief → righteousness → love → knowledge → abiding. Add them up and you have "the guard" against idols.

Here's a list of what John says should abide in the Christian and in what the Christian should abide:

In What We Abide	What Abides In Us
Jesus Christ, 2:6, 27, 28; 3:6, 24	Word of God, 2:14
The Light, 2:10	Love of the Father, 2:15
The church, 2:19	The gospel, 2:24
God, 4:13, 15, 16	The anointing, 2:27
	God's Seed, 3:9
	Christ, 3:24
	God, 4:12, 13, 15, 16.

Abide in Christ and you will abstain from idols.

121

THIRTEEN LESSONS ON I, II AND III JOHN

QUESTIONS FOR DISCUSSION:
1. How do water and blood bear witness to Jesus?
2. What do water and blood say about Jesus?
3. How does the message of water and blood communicate through us today? At what points are "water" and "blood" seen in our lives?
4. List specific ways the testimony Christians have in themselves is heard or seen.
5. List reasons why you know you are saved.
6. What understandings has the Son of God given us?
7. Is there eternal life outside of Jesus? Explain your answer.
8. Do we normally pray for an erring brother as we pray for a physically sick one? Why or why not?
9. Relate verse 21 to the rest of I John.
10. List as many ways to test Christianity from I John as possible. Now evaluate your maturity level in those areas. List specific ways you desire to become more Christlike.

II and III John

II and III John are the shortest writings in the Bible. However, congregational life will be significantly benefited when the principles in these two short letters are consistently practiced.

Throughout the two letters several identical concepts appear that connect the two in content. Here is a look at their content-connection.

Content	II John verse	III John verse
1. The author states his love for the reader with the same phrase — "I love in truth."	1	1
2. The recipients are "walking in truth"	4	3
3. Truth & love are related	3	4, 6
4. Christians walking in truth bring joy to other Christians	4	4
5. The recipients are loving the brethren	5	6
6. A warning against participating in evil	11	11
7. Hospitality discussed	10	5-10
8. Possibility of backsliding suggested	8-9	9
9. A reluctance to communicate further with pen & ink	12	13
10. A desire to speak to the reader face to face	13	14

THIRTEEN LESSONS ON I, II AND III JOHN

The two books also differ in several ways:

1. II John has no personal references, while III John does (v. 1, 9, 12).
2. II John includes a normal greeting for a letter (v. 3), while III John does not.
3. The readers of II John are warned to watch themselves lest they go too far (v. 9). The readers of III John are introduced to a person who has gone too far in at least one kind of behavior (v. 9).
4. II John warns against practicing hospitality on too broad a basis (vv. 10, 11). III John criticizes a person who doesn't practice hospitality on a broad enough basis (vv. 9, 10).

Perhaps point four is the major contrast to observe between the two letters and gives the church one of its most helpful lessons. The lesson is this: we are to practice hospitality to fellow Christians, but not on a wholesale basis. The way to protect ourselves from giving hospitality to the wrong persons is *not* by neglecting it for all persons. While II John stresses that all Christians are to participate in the reciprocating love — "love one another," III John contrasts a person who does love (1-8) with a person who will not allow Christians to do it (vv. 9-10).

II John stresses the fact that many deceivers are operating in the world (v. 7). III John names one dictator who is operating in the church (v. 9). Both the deceiver in the world and the dictator in the church accomplish the same goal. They both turn the eyes of their victims from the kind of conduct Jesus would manifest. Instead of turning Christians toward one another, they succeed in turning Christians against one another. Both the deceiver and dictator stand against truth and love. Both need to be exposed. To follow either is wrong.

Lesson Twelve
(II John)

WALKING IN TRUTH AND LOVE

  I. The Community of Walkers, vv. 1, 2
 II. The Contribution to the Walkers, v. 3
III. The Commendation of the Walkers, v. 4
 IV. The Commandments for the Walk, vv. 5, 6
  V. The Cautionary Walk, vv. 7-9
       A. Look Out for the Deceiver, v. 7
       B. Look Out for Yourselves, v. 8
       C. Look Out for the Correct Teaching, v. 9
 VI. The Constraints of the Walk, vv. 10, 11
VII. The Continuation of the Communications, vv. 12, 13

I. *The Community of Walkers,* vv. 1, 2

The elder to the chosen lady and her children, whom I love in truth; and not only I, but also all who know the truth, for the sake of the truth which abides in us and will be with us forever (vv. 1, 2).

The first verse gives us four problems about this short letter which cannot be objectively solved to the satisfaction of everyone. The first problem comes from the word **elder.** Was the writer writing from the stance of an older man or an officer in the church? The word "elder" (*presbuteros*) literally meant an older person (Luke 15:25; I Tim. 5:1, 2). But the word also referred to an official in the synagogue (Matt. 15:2) and in the church (Acts 11:30; 20:17). There is no clear-cut way to tell which designation John had in mind. He was an old man (in his nineties) when he wrote this letter; but we have no church historian that listed him as an elder in the church, although it would not be unusual for an apostle to be an elder (I Peter 5:1).

Who is the **chosen lady?** There are several suggestions:

1. An unnamed Christian woman.
2. A woman by the name of Kuria. The word "lady" comes from the Greek word *kuria*. Some think that is her proper name and should not be translated. Thus the text should read "to the chosen Kuria."
3. A woman by the name of Electa. The word "chosen" comes from this Greek word. Some feel that is her proper name and shouldn't be translated. Thus the text should read, "to the lady, Electa."
4. A woman by the name of Electa Kuria. Some feel that both of those Greek words are her proper name and neither should be translated.
5. Not a specific woman at all, but rather a symbolic way to refer to a congregation to which John was writing. Some of the argumentative support for this position follows:

    a. John would not have said to a woman, "whom I love in truth." This is an extremely weak argument. John would have had no more sexual connotations in saying this phrase than in using the same phrase for a man in III John 1. Don't forget, John is in his nineties, a model of Christian love, and an apostle for whom the Word and the concept of love were dominant in his writings.

    Some commentators who say John wouldn't admit love of a woman overlook the fact that John said he loved her *and* her children. The word **whom** I love is in masculine plural (*ous*) which includes the lady and her children of both sexes.

    b. Not everyone would love a specific woman, yet John said, "but also all who know the truth." This is also a weak argument, since we do not know who this woman is. She may have been so well known that such a statement could be made. It could be said of some individuals as well as of some congregations.

    c. John used the plural pronoun in referring to her in verses 8, 10, 12, but that's no problem when we remember that John wrote to the person *and* to her children.

II JOHN 1, 2

d. Designating the church with the symbol of a woman was not unusual. The Word for church (*ekklesia*) is the feminine gender. The church is referred to as a virgin (II Cor. 11:2), a bride (Eph. 5:22-32; Rev. 21:2, 9), as a mother (Gal. 4:26) and as a woman (Rev. 6:17). So it would have been quite in order for John to refer to the church as the elect or **chosen lady**. If Jesus is the Kurios (Master), the church is His Kuria (mistress, which is what the word really means).

If Gaius is an individual in III John (and all commentators agree that he is) it would not be unusual for *kuria* (translated lady) to be an individual in II John, for the two letters begin in the same manner. The main difference between the beginning of the two is the name of the person and an adjective describing that person. But both adjectives describe an activity of God which has resulted in that individual being a Christian. Here's a comparison of the two beginnings:

II John - the elder to the chosen kuria whom I love in truth.

III John - the elder to the beloved Gaius whom I love in truth.

"And her children" has been omitted in order to see the comparison better. If *kuria* (lady) is the church, why add "and her children"? Doesn't the church include *all* the members?

Whether or not John first addressed this to a Christian individual or to a Christian congregation makes no difference when it comes to its application. If to an individual, its teaching applies to the whole church. If to a church, its teaching applies to each individual.

Who are **her children**? The answer to that depends upon who the lady is. If she is an individual, **her children** are her offspring (I Tim. 3:4). If she is a congregation, **her children** are the members (Gal. 4:19, 25).

What does it mean to **love in truth**? It could mean one of two things — truly loving, which stressed the sincerity of the love (I Cor. 5:8; Matt. 22:16; John 4:23) or loving "in Christ," that is, as a Christian who is positioned in Christ. Several times Jesus is referred to as "the truth" (John 14:6). To walk "in the truth" is to walk "in Christ"; to love "in the truth" is to love "in Christ," to believe "in the truth" is to believe "in Christ."

Some suggest the absence of the article here prevents John from referring to Christ. But that's not necessarily so. The Greeks often eliminated the article for emphasis when a preposition was used. It seems that **in truth** in II John refers to the same thing that "in the truth" refers to (vv. 1, 2, 3, 4). I lean toward the position that in each case **truth** refers to Jesus Christ.

v. 1 love in truth . . . . love in Christ
know the truth . . . . know Christ

THIRTEEN LESSONS ON I, II AND III JOHN

v. 2 for the sake of the truth . . . . for the sake of Christ
which abides in us and who abides with us
will be with us forever (John 14) and abides
with us forever (Matt. 28:20).
v. 3 in truth . . . . in Christ
v. 4 walking in truth . . . . walking in Christ (I John 2:6; Col. 2:6).

The person (lady) or group of persons (church) must have been well known as well as respected for John said, **whom I love in truth; and not only I, but also all who love the truth.** Here is a picture of fellowship in the family of God that is not dampened by distance. Somehow we must restore the New Testament concept that takes seriously a world-wide kinship with all Christians. The New Testament does not heighten the local autonomy of a body of believers to the exclusion of Christians who belong to another "flock." When we are a part of the body of Christ, we are connected to *all* the other parts.

We must all evaluate whether or not our congregational actions show that essential and functioning unity. For instance, does your congregation charge Christians of another congregation to use your building for a wedding or a funeral but does not charge its own members? What does that communicate about our functional unity? To rationalize such action because of economics and membership support does very little to communicate the unity in the church which is different from the unity in the world. Perhaps each member of the church should memorize Socrates' response when he was asked about his citizenship. He would not narrow his citizenship to one location lest be begin to think too narrowly about others. He would simply reply, "I am a citizen of the world." Perhaps we should talk more about being a member of *the church* than of the First _____ church at _____. Wasn't that what Paul was saying when he wrote to the church at Corinth? "To the church of God which is at Corinth, to those who have been sanctified in Christ Jesus, saints by calling, *with all who in every place call upon the name of our Lord Jesus Christ, their Lord and ours* (I Cor. 1:2).

To know the truth is to know Jesus Christ who is the truth. That provides the common ground for loving another Christian who may or may not be known well. While knowing Christ is the ground or basis for loving another Christian, Christ is also the purpose for such love, **for the sake of the truth.** Christ came for the purpose of uniting us (Eph. 1:9-10; 2:11-21). To love another Christian is to live for the sake of Christ's purpose. And we can do it because He (the truth) **abides in us** through the Holy Spirit and **will be with us forever** as He promised (Matt. 28:20).

Connecting the concepts of "abiding," "loving," and "Christ" was common for John (John 14:17; 15:4-16; I John 2:6-28; 3:6, 17, 24; 4:12-16).

II. *The Contribution to the Walkers,* v. 3

Grace, mercy and peace will be with us, from God the Father and from Jesus Christ, the Son of the Father, in truth and love (v. 3).

God equips us to walk the way He expects us to walk. His contribution to our life-style involves His grace (His activities for our good), His mercy (His attitude for our good), and His peace (His effect for our good). God's mercy and grace are twin characteristics of His active compassion for our benefit (Eph. 2:4, 7-8). Peace (harmony or total well-being) is the result of His grace and mercy. If we are to beam peace to others, we must offer it in the same package God offers it to us — grace, mercy, truth, and love. Notice the connection of **truth and love.** John will continue that connection (vv. 4-6).

III. *The Commendation of the Walkers,* v. 4

I was very glad to find some of your children walking in truth, just as we have received commandment to do from the Father (v. 4).

There is joy in serving Jesus, but it isn't joy that's restricted to only the people who are serving. Serving Christians also bring joy to others who hear about it. The aged John was delighted to hear that Christians were walking as Christ walked (v. 4, III John 3). This corresponds with what John wrote about joy in his first epistle (I John 1:4). To **walk in the truth** is to walk in Jesus who is the truth (John 14:6). The **commandment** we have received **from the Father** is to walk as Christ walked (Col. 2:6; I John 2:6) which included love (John 13:34-35; 15:10-12).

But truth is not for just knowing, but also for doing. It doesn't involve just content for memory, but also commandments for morals.

IV. *The Commandments for the Walk,* vv. 5, 6

And now I ask you, lady, not as writing to you a new commandment, but the one which we have had from the beginning, that we love one another. And this is love, that we walk according to His commandments. This is the commandment, just as you have heard from the beginning, that you should walk in it (vv. 5, 6).

John identified the commandment they had from the Father — **that we love one another.** (For a discussion of the words "new" and "from the beginning" see I John 2:7-8.) John didn't ask them to *start* loving one another but to *continue* doing it (*agapomen-*present subjunctive).

The singular **commandment** is the summation of God's commands while the plural **commandments** are the specific ways to love. Several times John moved from the singular commandment to the plural commandments in making this point (John 13:34; 14:15; 15:12; I John 2:3-4,

7-8; 3:22-24; 5:2-3). Both Jesus and Paul had summed up many specific commandments into the one — love (Matt. 22:34-40; Rom. 13:8-10). There is not one specific commandment of God that isn't wrapped up in the package of love and doesn't help us with the practice of loving. To walk in the truth (v. 1) is to walk **according to His commandments.** To walk according to His commandments is to walk according to love. **Love** here is *agape*-love, which is always the unselfish love of meeting another person's need for his well-being. It thinks of the other person first, and it acts for the other person first.

But why did John feel the need to encourage his readers to continue doing something that they had evidently made a habit pattern to do so well? There was a situation in the world that he did not want to infiltrate into the churches. He outlined the problems and the potential danger of it in the next five verses. Christians can never cease to be cautious when they live in this world.

V. *The Cautionary Walk,* vv. 7-9

  A. *Look Out for the Deceiver,* v. 7

For many deceivers have gone out into the world, those who do not acknowledge Jesus Christ as coming in the flesh. This is the deceiver and the antichrist (v. 7).

This verse gives the reason for John's admonition for their continuation. **For** (*hoti* — because) **many deceivers have gone out into the world.** John didn't just say that many deceivers were in the world, but that they had **gone out into the world.** From where did they go out? Evidently John had in mind some people who had been in the church (I John 2:19; 4:1). Some have since **gone out** of the church and *into* the world. Paul wrote that some would be from among the elders (Acts 20:28-31).

A deceiver is someone who leads others astray. The word comes from the same word as the English word for planet (*planos*). As a planet is a wandering body *above* the earth, so a deceiver (*planos*) is a wandering body *on* the earth. He isn't anchored to the Rock of Ages. So he tries to unanchor others. He does it by turning people's minds from Jesus and encouraging them to doubt Him, so that they **do not acknowledge Jesus Christ as coming in the flesh.**

The word **acknowledge** is the word for confess (*homologeo*) which means to "speak like." They do not speak about Jesus as the Father does or Jesus Himself does. They are against Jesus being the anointed Christ and thus are called the antichrists. (See also comments on I John 2:18, 22; 4:3).

We have hurt the family of God by equating these deceivers to anybody who doesn't agree with us in every aspect of doctrine. We are to love fellow Christians not because we agree on everything but in spite of it. However, our love is not to wear blinders.

II JOHN 7, 8

Christians can be led astray. If they couldn't it would be useless to look out for the deceivers. If a Christian cannot be lured into denying Jesus, John wrote this caution to the wrong people. To deny that Jesus came in the flesh is to make God a liar (I John 5:10), and to deny that Jesus died for us, that He rose bodily, that He will return, the witness of the apostles and prophets, and that He can live in our flesh through the Holy Spirit. This last point may be the teaching John had in mind. In I John he certainly spotlighted the fact that Jesus came in the flesh in the past, but in this verse the present tense is used for the verb **coming**.

After denying that Jesus ever came in the flesh (I John 2:18, 22; 4:2, 3), it is just a logical jump to conclude that He is not presently coming into the flesh of men via the Holy Spirit. If that is denied, ethics is reduced to humanism. That is precisely what Gnosticism did to ethics in the first century. If there is no Divine that comes into the human, the human becomes his own god.

B. *Look Out for Yourselves*, v. 8

Watch yourselves, that you might not lose what we have accomplished, but that you may receive a full reward (v. 8).

Watch (*blepo*) has the idea of being careful. If Christians could not be affected by the deceiver, John would not have written this. Christians are commanded to be careful. Every time this command was used the situation was real. To suggest that Christians can't be deceived is obviously erroneous. Here are the places where this cautionary command is used (note *blepo* is translated many different ways):

The Command (*blepo*)	*The Caution*
1. See to it (Mark. 13:5)	No one misleads you
2. Be on your guard (Mark. 13:9)	People will oppose the apostles
3. Take heed (Mark 13:23	False Christs and prophets will try to lead the elect astray
4. Take heed (Mark 13:33)	Jesus will return
5. Take care (Luke 8:18)	All will be revealed
6. See to it (Luke 21:8)	Many will come to mislead
7. Take heed (Acts 13:40)	Prophets will be fulfilled
8. Consider (I Cor. 1:26)	Not many wise are called
9. Take care (I Cor. 8:9)	One person's liberty can be a stumbling block to another

THIRTEEN LESSONS ON I, II AND III JOHN

10. Look (I Cor. 10:18) .... An example
11. See that (I Cor. 16:10) .... Timothy isn't afraid
12. Take care (Gal. 5:15) .... Lest you be consumed by one another
13. Be careful (Eph. 5:15) .... Your walk
14. Beware (Phil. 3:2) .... False teachers
15. See to it (Col. 2:8) .... Lest someone takes you captive through philosophy and empty deception
16. Take heed (Col. 4:1) .... About ministry which God gave
17. Take care (Heb. 3:12) .... About falling away
18. See to it (Heb. 12:25) .... Refuse warnings
19. Watch (II John 8) .... Might lose reward

Notice that every other usage of this command in this exact form (*blepete*) spotlights a real possibility. There is no objective reason to suggest that the Christian cannot lose what He has accomplished. He can. That's why John issued the warning. The doctrine of eternal security is found wanting with careful holistic study of God's Word.

What is it that can be lost? **What we have accomplished** can be lost. The deceivers who deny Jesus (v. 7) lure us into their camp. We lose what acknowledging Christ gains—eternal life. Some suggest that we merely lose the **full reward** but not eternal life, but that seems doubtful. It is true that our reward (*misthos*) can be lost if we build an inferior product on the foundation (I Cor. 3:12-15). But I Cor. 3 and II John 7-8 are talking about two different topics entirely. I Cor. 3 is discussing building on the foundation, thus Jesus is still acknowledged. But II John 7-8 is discussing the elimination of the foundation—the foundation is not acknowledged, let alone built upon.

   C. *Look Out for the Correct Teaching*, v. 9

Any one who goes too far and does not abide in the teaching of Christ, does not have God; the one who abides in the teaching, he has both the Father and the Son (v. 9).

John is no respecter of persons. Consequently, he emphasized that **anyone** regardless of church status, degrees, or intellect who **goes too far does not have God**. But when does a person **go too far**? Anyone goes **too far** when he **does not abide in the teaching of Christ**. That could mean the teaching *from* Christ (subjective genitive) or the teaching *about* Christ (objective genitive). There is no need to argue the point. In the context, either the teaching *from* Christ or the teaching *about* Christ would be proper, for they both refer to the fact that Jesus came and still comes (verse 7). To deny those facts is to **go too far** (*proago* — literally go ahead or lead ahead). The person who **goes too far** is trying to be more "advanced" than God is.

While Gnosticism claimed to have a corner on intellectualism in the first century, much modern theology does the same thing today. I have read many theologians who say that the Biblical claims about Jesus' divinity in human form were unsophisticated, simplistic descriptions that the modern man who has "come of age" cannot accept. They conclude that the miracle of Jesus (the virgin's conception) and the miracles from Jesus have to be scientifically explained. Those who think in this way have gone beyond the spiritual precipice. They **do not have God.** As long as they remain ahead of God, they have become their own gods. And in that state, they are lost. For to be without the Son is to be without the Father and eternal life (I John 5:12).

But the one who abides in the doctrine about Jesus **has both the Father and the Son.** To have one is to have the other (John 14:6; John 3:36; 5:23; 8:19; 14:7, 9; 16:3).

VI. *The Constraints of the Walk,* vv. 10, 11

> **If any one comes to you and does not bring this teaching, do not receive him into your house, and do not give him a greeting; for the one who gives him a greeting participates in his evil deeds (vv. 10, 11).**

John put a curb upon their loving one another. Because of the end result of those who deny Jesus (vv. 7-9), John wrote a command against any material support that would help advance the continuation of that teaching.

In the first century, religious teachers travelled widely without the aid of motorized homes or campers. One logistical problem centered around a place to stay while enroute. The inns were notorious for being dens of iniquity that offered little opportunity for sleep. Not only were they immoral and noisy, but also dirty and insect-infested. Consequently, Christians early adopted the practice of opening their homes to their travelling brothers and sisters in Christ. Not only did it provide a ministry to the traveller, but the fellowship provided a ministry to the hosts. This practice of caring for travellers goes back as far as Abraham (Gen. 18:1-8). In fact, it goes as far back as God promising to protect Cain as he travelled (Gen. 4:14, 15).

Being hospitable to strangers is a characteristic of God that His people should duplicate. It is a character trait expected of an elder (I Tim. 3:2; Titus 1:8), and it is to be expressed by all Christians (Rom. 12:13; Heb. 13:2; I Pet. 4:9). It was one of the immediate results of people converted to Jesus (Acts 10:48; 16:15; 16:33, 34). Jesus expected that God's people would care for the travelling apostles (Matt. 10:11-13). Those who would give even a cup of water would be rewarded by God (Matt. 10:40-42). Every Christian home was also a Christian "inn" in the first century. What a beautiful expression of unity.

But that kind of hospitality had some restrictions attached to it. John commanded that Christians should not take in those whose teachings denied the divine incarnation of Jesus. **If anyone comes to you** refers to the travellers who wanted bed and board. **Does not bring this teaching** refers to the teaching about Christ (v. 9) which affirms His divine incarnation (v. 7). **Do not receive him into your house** refers to the room and board. **Do not give him a greeting** refers to recognizing him as a brother and greeting him as such. To *greet* him as a brother would carry the responsibility to *treat* him as a brother which would involve providing him a base of operation while he's in town — room and board. The doors were to be locked to such people.

Some commentators say such actions would be cruel and non-Christian. But it is neither. Nothing is cruel and non-Christian when commanded by God. This type of treatment is mild compared to the devastating end-result of these false teachers (vv. 8, 9). The treatment is also mild compared to Paul's and Jesus' commands:

> But even though we, or an angel from heaven, should preach to you a gospel contrary to that which we have preached to you, let him be accursed. As we have said before, so I say again now, if any man is preaching to you a gospel contrary to that which you received, let him be accursed (Gal. 1:8, 9).

> Would that those who are troubling you would even mutilate themselves (Gal. 5:12).

> But whoever causes one of these little ones who believe in Me to stumble, it is better for him that a heavy millstone be hung around his neck, and that he be drowned in the depth of the sea (Matt. 18:6).

C. H. Dodd claims that John's restriction was not necessary nor right. However, we cannot take John 3:16-18, 14:6, and I John 5:12 seriously and claim that supporting antichrists is the right thing to do.

While Dodd is too lenient with this command, some are too rigid. They claim that this command prohibits allowing false teachers from coming inside your house. These verses do not propel us into a life of total isolation. They prevent us from supporting the teaching of the false propagandists. We must show them that we can love them as people without supporting them as teachers. That may require that we have them in our houses so *we* can teach *them*. If we have them in our home for a meal today, it isn't to provide part of their salary. Remember, the situation is different. To **receive them** in the first century meant to give them provisions so

II JOHN 10-13

their ministry could continue. *It is support that is prohibited, not acquaintance with them.* We are to give them absolutely no material provisions in return for their "spiritual" services. But we are to fulfill Matt. 28:19-20 with them.

Also some have been too rigid with these verses by applying them to anyone not in "our" group. John was talking about not supporting the *antichrists.* He was not referring to cutting off relations with Christian brothers and sisters whose understanding doesn't square exactly with ours.

Quite early some decided to not allow hospitality to any travelling Christians. That way the church could be innocent of even unknowingly supporting antichrists. We will see such a person in III John. But he's as perverted as the deceivers in II John.

VII. *The Continuation of the Communication,* vv. 12, 13

Having many things to write to you, I do not want to do so with paper and ink; but I hope to come to you and speak face to face, that your joy may be made full. The children of your chosen sister greet you (vv. 12, 13).

Even though in his nineties, John had not yet retired from Christian service. He still had much to teach others. Evidently he didn't consider himself retired from travelling either — **I hope to come to you.** What a beautiful attitude!

It may be possible that John sensed more potential danger in the church than he had clearly indicated. The phrase **face to face** comes from the words for "mouth to mouth" (*stoma*). Sometimes that Greek word for "mouth" was used when personal persuasion was deemed necessary. However, John probably was only thinking about a personal visit in which his teachings would help complete their joy. How would it do that? The same way his writings would (I John 1:4) — by enhancing their Christlikeness and fellowship with each other (I John 1:3-4).

John closed his letter with a greeting from others — **the children of your chosen sister greet you.** If the "chosen lady" (v. 1) was an individual, then her nieces and nephews are in John's presence. If the "chosen lady" is the church, then the **children of her chosen sister** are the members of another assembly. But that's a bit awkward. Why not just say her chosen sister (a sister congregation) greets you? Either way, the "lady" was not alone in the world. People knew her and cared for her, although they didn't live close to her. She needed them, and so do we all. Let's live like it.

QUESTIONS FOR DISCUSSION:

1 What do you do that would cause others to say that you walk in the truth?

THIRTEEN LESSONS ON I, II AND III JOHN

2. What do you do that might cause some to wonder about whether you do walk in the truth or not?
3. List modern-day antichrists.
4. How can a Christian go too far?
5. Relate verse 9 with I John 5:12. How does abiding in the teaching fit?
6. What did verses 10-11 mean in the first century? How can it be applied today?

Lesson Thirteen
(III John)

PRACTICING HOSPITALITY

I. A Respected Model — Gaius, vv. 1-8
   A. His Soul Prospers, vv. 1, 2
   B. His "Smiles" Multiply, vv. 3, 4
      1. What? vv. 5, 6
      2. Why? vv. 7, 8
II. A Revolting Model — Diotrephes, vv. 9, 10
   A. His Perverted Priority, v. 9
   B. His Perverted Practices, v. 10
III. A Recommendation, vv. 11, 12
   A. For a Practice of God, v. 11
   B. For a Person of God, v. 12
IV. A Resolution, vv. 13, 14

    The quantitative measurement of a writing does not reflect its quality or depth. Abraham Lincoln's Gettysburg Address has outlived many longer political speeches. Neither can the significance of God's teaching be measured by how long it takes to read it or hear it. III John is a neglected letter in Christianity, probably because of its brevity. We have failed to realize the richness of God's teaching in those few words. Consequently, we have permitted the modern clones of Diotrephes to multiply; and at the same time, not honored the Gaiuses of our day as we should.

I. *A Respected Model — Gaius, vv. 1-8*

  A. *His Soul Prospers, vv. 1, 2*

The elder to the beloved Gaius, whom I love in truth. Beloved, I pray that in all respects you may prosper and be in good health, just as your soul prospers (vv. 1-2).

The elder (see note on II John 1) was neither too old nor too busy to write a Christian brother a commendation about his conduct which had received criticism and probably excommunication from the church (v. 10).

We do not know exactly who Gaius was, but that was a popular name in the first century. Some even suggest that it was the most common of all names in the Roman Empire. But that's not an objective statement unless we had all the names in the Roman Empire preserved, which we don't. However, we do know about several Gaiuses in the New Testament (Acts 19:29; 20:4; Rom. 16:23; I Cor. 1:14). Although we do not know *who* Gaius is, we know *how* he is and *what* he did.

How is he? He is **beloved** by God, loved by John **whom I love in truth** (see note on II John 1), prayed for (v. 2), respected by the church (v. 6), and his soul was prospering (v. 2).

The word **prosper** (*euodoomai*) literally means "good journey." His soul was having such a "good journey" through this life that John prayed ("wished" — *euchomai*) that in every way his physical health might experience the same "good journey" through life, (note: **good** and **prosper** are the same Greek words) as his soul was experiencing.

Why did John wish good health for Gaius? Just to save doctor bills? No! John hoped that this kind of model might continue and inspire others in the church to follow suit (v. 11). Wouldn't it be great if our souls were always in better health than our physical bodies? Do we spend more time, energy, and money trying to keep the body in shape without a significant purpose? From Gaius, we learn that the soul prospers as the soul practices unselfishness. The soul is that aspect of our lives that is not destroyed when the body is (Matt. 10:28).

II. *His "Smiles" Multiply, vv. 3, 4*

For I was very glad when brethren came and bore witness to your truth, that is, how you are walking in truth. I have no greater joy than this to hear of my children walking in the truth (vv. 3, 4).

"There is joy in serving Jesus" is more than words in a chorus. It is the truth in a Christian. The joy of a Christian cannot be contained. It operates on a domino principle — it triggers the joy of other Christians.

III JOHN 3, 4

What is the thought that gave a ninety-year-old John the greatest joy? The thought that he will soon be in heaven? No! The thought that he has fought the good fight? No! The thought that his responsibilities for God are now behind him? No! What is it then? **I have no greater joy than this, to hear of my children walking in the truth.** What an unselfish source of joy! He is the happiest when he sees other people happy. Evidently Gaius was a convert of John because of John's use of the words, **my children.** Evangelists often referred to their converts as their children (I Cor. 4:17; Gal. 4:19; I Tim. 1:2, 18; II Tim. 1:2; Philemon 10).

We learn something important about evangelism in the early church from this verse. The early evangelists were not just concerned with new births. They also maintained an intimate concern for the spiritual well-being of their converts. A good father never aborts his concern for a new babe after the baby has been delivered. The concern remains through the development of that baby. That's an apostolic model that deserves repeating today.

There's another truth we can learn from these verses. John shared with Gaius the good reports he had heard about Gaius **walking in the truth** (see II John 4), **your truth** (v. 2), and **your love** (v. 6). How easy it is to neglect to do that. We have piously patted ourselves on the back for not praising anyone but God. But in doing that we have neglected some significant biblical teachings, such as giving preference to one another in honor (Rom. 12:10), giving honor to whom honor is due (Rom. 13:7), share words that can "give grace to those who hear" (Eph. 4:29), and be kind to one another (Eph. 4:32). Paul made it a practice to praise the unselfish ministry of others (Rom. 16; I Tim. 16:10; Phil. 1:3-5; 2:19-30; Col. 1:3-7; 4:10-14; I Thess. 1; 3:1-2; II Thess. 1:3-4; I Tim. 1:2; II Tim. 1:3-5; 4:11; Titus 3:12-14; Philemon 4-7, 11).

Christians need to be converted from two extremes—stingy praise and extravagant praise. Both can damage a person. There is so much in the world that throws a damper upon unselfish discipleship that we should not add to it by forbidding that verbal admiration and thankfulness be uttered to another. Right now is a good time to write a note or phone a person with a word of gratitude for his service in the family of God.

Some of the people who are the least thanked are those who have never written one word for publication or never sat on a platform. Gaius represented them. He was not an "out front" person, but he habitually opened his home and pocketbook to travelling preachers. Don't you have people like that in your church? Don't you have those people whom others say only good things about? Why allow all that to be said behind their backs? Why wait until the funeral to send the flowers?

THIRTEEN LESSONS ON I, II AND III JOHN

Gaius and everyone like him make life joyous for others in the church. We can spread either gladness or sadness through the church by our attitudes and examples.

   C. *His Services Promoted,* v. 5-8

      1. What? vv. 5, 6

> **Beloved, you are acting faithfully in whatever you accomplish for the brethren, and especially when they are strangers: and they bear witness to your love before the church; and you will do well to send them on their way in a manner worthy of God (vv. 5, 6).**

What did Gaius do? Three times in five verses John called Gaius **beloved.** Aren't you overdoing it, John? No, not at all. If we look at what Diotrephes was doing to Gaius (v. 10), then we can see why Gaius needed to hear the apostle say more than once, **beloved.** While Diotrephes was condemning the thing Gaius was doing, John commended him. While Diotrephes caused factions in what he was *not* accomplishing for the brethren, Gaius was **acting faithfully in whatever** he was **accomplishing for the brethren,** especially **strangers.** In fact, he was doing for **strangers** what Diotrephes was not even doing for local members of the fellowship.

But what was Gaius doing **for the brethren and especially when they are strangers?** He was hospitable to them. Holiness and hospitality go together. Hospitality (*philoxenos*) literally means love (*philos*) to strangers (*xenos*). The word for love (*philos*) stresses the friendship-kind of love. Hospitality involves being friendly with strangers. There are many different objects a person can love with *philos*-love. He can love words or logic (*philologos*), arguments (*philoneikos*), to be first (*philoproteuo*), wisdom (*philosophia*), children (*philoteknos*), honor (*philotimeomai*), music (*philharmonic*), men (*philanthropy*), brothers (*philadelphia*) and Greeks (*philhelene*). But none of these so marks the Christian as the *philoxenos*—a lover of strangers. God expects Christians to be hospitable.

> Contributing to the needs of the saints, practicing *hospitality* (Rom. 12:13).

> An overseer, then, must be above reproach, the husband of one wife, temperate, prudent, respectable, *hospitable,* able to teach (I Tim. 3:2).

> Let a widow be put on the list only if she is not less than sixty years old, having been the wife of one man, having a reputation for good works; and if she has brought up children, if she has shown *hospitality* to strangers, if she has washed the saints' feet, if she has assisted those in distress, and if she has devoted herself to every good work (I Tim. 5:9, 10).

For the overseer must be above reproach, as God's steward, not self-willed, not quick-tempered, not addicted to wine, not pugnacious, not fond of sordid gain, but *hospitable,* loving what is good, sensible, just, devout, self-controlled (Titus 1:7, 8).

Do not neglect to show *hospitality* to strangers, for by this some have entertained angels without knowing it (Hebrews 13:2).

Be *hospitable* to one another without complaint (I Pet. 4:9).

Although the *philos* kind of love stresses a friendly kind of love, hospitality can never be fulfilled by only a friendly greeting. It always includes taking care of needs. In the first century, it involved inviting travelling Christians into one's home and to one's table.

One of the ways Christianity spread in the first century was through the preaching of travelling evangelists. Inns were degrading, dirty, and morally deplorable places to stay (see introduction to II & III John), and they cost a lot of money. God expected the church to provide for travelling missionaries, and that was what Gaius was doing. John wrote, he was doing **well to send them on their way.** That involved not only providing room and board while they were in the area, but also enough money and/or food for them to reach their next destination. To **send** literally means to "send ahead" (*propempo*).

It's one thing to send them on their way. But it's another thing to do it **in a manner worthy of God.** How we would send God on His way is how we should send His ministers on their way. Would we send God away empty-handed? But why would John use the phrase **worthy of God?** Because the way we treat God's people is the way we treat God. Jesus especially applied that truth to the treatment of those who preached (Matt. 10:9-14, 40-42; John 13:20). Be careful how you treat preachers. God takes it personally.

2. Why? vv. 7, 8

For they went out for the sake of the name, accepting nothing from the Gentiles. Therefore we ought to support such men, that we may be fellow-workers with the truth (vv. 7-8).

The word for (*gar*) explains why hospitality should be given to God's preachers. They were serving God **(for the sake of the name)** without material support from the non-Christians — **accepting nothing from the Gentiles.** If they accepted nothing from the non-Christians, there is only one source left — the Christians. **Therefore we** (Christians) **ought to support such men.** The word **support** (*hupolambano*) literally means to "take under." Christians should *take* God's spokesmen *under* their care. That isn't an option, but an obligation. The word **ought** (*opheilo*) stresses a debt. Christians owe material aid to those persons who give their wage-earning time to serving the church and the world with the ministry of God.

> And let the one who is taught the word share all good things with him who teaches (Gal. 6:6).

> Who at any time serves as a soldier at his own expense? Who plants a vineyard, and does not eat the fruit of it? Or who tends a flock and does not use the milk of the flock? (I Cor. 9:7).

> If we sowed spiritual things in you, is it too much if we should reap material things from you? (I Cor. 9:11)

> So also the Lord directed those who proclaim the gospel to get their living from the gospel (I Cor. 9:14).

> Yes, they were pleased to do so, and they are indebted to them. For if the Gentiles have shared in their spiritual things, they are indebted to minister to them also in material things (Rom. 15:27).

To do that is to become **fellow workers with the truth.** Financially supporting ministers of the Word does not fulfill our own ministry, but it does make us participating partners with their ministry which multiplies ours. Investing in the ministry of others, while ministering ourselves, allows us to receive the dividends of whatever they invest into kingdom service. That's why Paul wrote to a supporting congregation, "Not that I seek the gift itself, but I seek for the profit which increases to your account" (Phil. 4:17).

I wonder how many congregations or individuals are sitting on large savings accounts while Christian work goes begging? It's easy to adopt and maintain a "depression-mentality" — that is, keeping church funds secured for tough times. That's the life of fear. The life of faith believes the Bible when it says:

> Now He who supplies seed to the sower and bread for food, will supply and multiply your seed for sowing and increase the harvest of your righteousness; you will be enriched in everything for all liberality, which through us is producing thanksgiving to God. For the ministry of this service is not fully supplying the needs of the saints, but is also overflowing through many thanksgivings to God. Because of the proof given by this ministry they will glorify God for your obedience to your confession of the gospel of Christ, and for the liberality of your contribution to them and to all, while they also, by prayer on your behalf, yearn for you because of the surpassing grace of God in you. Thanks be to God for His indescribable gift! (II Cor. 9:10-15).

God intends for the senders and the sent ones to be continually connected to each other. Neither has the right to neglect the other. The preacher or missionary has no right to keep his needs secret. And the church has no right to fuss about every pay raise. We may all be shocked at God's displeasure at us for fussing so much about the pay of the preachers. We don't do that about the pay of pilots, pharmacists, publishers, professors, printers, planners, planters, painters, philosophers, etc. Where are our values? It's not as big a step as we may think from being disparaging and derogatory about missionary and preacher support to becoming a modern Diotrephes.

II. *A Revolting Model — Diotrephes,* vv. 9, 10

The cliché, "the wheel that squeaks gets the grease" was followed in John's day as it is now. Diotrephes was a "big wheel" who squeaked loudly. The people catered to him. But John pulled the rug out from underneath him in this letter.

Diotrephes may be the oldest person who has ever lived. From one perspective, its difficult to think that he ever died. He seems to not only be eternal — for all times, but also omnipresent — in all places. But why not? He was evidently a pawn of the Devil and didn't know it. Of course he died, but his attitude lives on. If you doubt that, just preach about Diotrephes and notice how many people will take it personally. A. T. Robertson reported that he wrote an article about Diotrephes for a denominational paper. After the paper came out, twenty-five church officers cancelled the paper in protest, because they thought the paper was attacking them personally.

The problem of Diotrephes was twofold: a wrong priority and wrong practices. Both are related to each other.

A. *His Perverted Priority,* v. 9

I wrote something to the church; but Diotrephes, who loves to be first among them, does not accept what we say (v. 9).

Diotrephes was a revolting model of hospitality and of Christian leadership *per se* because **he loves to be first.** He had observed how leaders in the world become **first** and so acted as they did. He became a dictator over his Christian peers. By doing that he became the opposite of a great person in the Kingdom:

> But Jesus called them to Himself, and said, "You know that the rulers of the Gentiles lord it over them, and their great men exercise authority over them. It is not so among you, but whoever wishes to become great among you shall be your servant, and whoever wishes to be first among you shall be your slave" (Matt. 20:25-27).

How long will it take us to reject the philosophy of Diotrephes and accept the philosophy of Jesus?

THIRTEEN LESSONS ON I, II AND III JOHN

Diotrephes was so hooked on himself that he wouldn't even accept the authority of an apostle — **I wrote something to the church; but Diotrephes . . . does not accept what we say.** Diotrephes didn't just *want* to be first, he already thought he *was* first and loved it. No one is more arrogant than the one who will not be taught by another. The more closed-minded a person is, the more infallible he thinks he is. And the more infallible he thinks he is, the more inflexible he is. The more inflexible he is, the more impossible he becomes. The more impossible he becomes, the more he thinks he is like God — and acts like a god, but certainly not like *the* God who loves and serves.

What did John write that Diotrephes rejected? We can't be certain. However, in light of the immediate context, he may have written about supporting a preacher through hospitality. He might even have praised a list of people who had practiced hospitality — the same people Diotrephes kicked out of the church (v. 10).

B. *His Perverted Practices*, v. 10

For this reason, if I come, I will call attention to his deeds which he does, unjustly accusing us with wicked words: and not satisfied with this, neither does he himself receive the brethren, and he forbids those who desire to do so, and puts them out of the church (v. 10).

Diotrephes' perverted practices included: (1) rejecting apostolic teaching when it didn't jibe with his, (2) unjustly slandering others — even the apostles, (3) refusing to be hospitable, (4) forbidding the church to practice hospitality, (5) excommunicating those who were hospitable.

Diotrephes may have begun his practice of no hospitality as a result of some bitter experiences. It is true that some travelling teachers, missionaries, preachers, etc., take advantage of hospitality by lining their pockets. "Love offerings" can be very lucrative. Some were no doubt in Christian service just for the money. Some had even charged Paul with that motive. On occasion he felt the need to write that he never travelled and preached "with a pretext for greed" (I Thess. 2:5), "For we are not like many, peddling the Word of God, but as from sincerity, but as from God, we speak in Christ in the sight of God" (II Cor. 2:17).

Because some people may take advantage of the grace and trust of the church does not give us a right to set up a censureship against all people involved in similar ministries. That's the bureaucracy mentality of big government which has no place in the Christian Church. Because some music groups may have left a bad impression does not give us a mandate to ban all music groups. Because a graduate from one college or seminary was a total disappointment doesn't mean we cut off that college's support, etc.

Not only did Diotrephes not accept what John said, he tried to discredit John's reputation by **unjustly accusing with wicked words.** The words **unjustly accuse** (*phluareo*) refers to nonsense talk. His accusations didn't make sense, but they made noise. And that's what he wanted.

Diotrephes was a man who was very threatened. A person who is threatened by others will usually use derogatory remarks about those who threaten him and stay aloof from fellowshipping with them — **puts them out.** Why would Diotrephes refuse to practice hospitality? The answer is obvious. If the travelling evangelists were mature in character and taught the church members how to fellowship properly, the character and teachings of Diotrephes would be shown up for the sham they were. The members would soon discover that Diotrephes didn't have all the answers after all. So Diotrephes tried to protect himself by being a schemer, designing activities that kept him on top. What a perverted Christian!

The Diotrephes-mentality lives on. It can invade and infest any church or Christian institution. It always stifles freedom and weakens interpersonal trust in one another. Diotrephes knew that *he* couldn't be trusted, so he didn't trust others. His policies did more checking up on people than trusting them. Anytime this develops, fellowship is fragmented in the body of Christ.

The Diotrephes-mentality is a tragedy. But an equal tragedy is the church's or institution's tendency to let it go so the "boat won't get rocked." Isn't it better to "rock the boat" than let it sink? John was courageous enough to expose Diotrephes with the promise that he would follow it up with a personal visit in which he would **call attention to his deeds.** The Diotrephes-kind of people must not go unchecked. Their kind of leaven can leaven the whole lump. The church has an apostolic mandate to expel the factious person (Titus 3:10).

III. *A Recommendation,* vv. 11, 12

   A. *For a Practice of God,* v. 11

> **Beloved, do not imitate what is evil, but what is good. The one who does good is of God; the one who does evil has not seen God (v. 11).**

In this context the **evil** which is not to be imitated is the Diotrephes-mentality. However, it is sad that it is imitated, for often the Diotrephes-people get their way. Followers soon learn that to get their way, they need to become a Diotrephes. That modeling of evil must cease.

The **good** is the Gaius-mentality. Gaius had a correct head and a warm heart. He had a balance of *grace* and *truth* as did Jesus (John 1:14), and as the church is to continuously demonstrate (Eph. 4:15). To imitate

Gaius' hospitality is to be **of God,** for God is love (I John 4:1-7). And to be **of God** is to be like God (I John 3:10; 4:4, 6; 5:19). Those who are like Diotrephes have so missed the character of God that John says they have **not seen God.**

We see God in Jesus. Just try to find Jesus' conduct in Diotrephes. It can't be done. Remember I John 3:21 — "Guard yourselves from idols"? Don't let Diotrephes become an idol just because his tactics seem to work. The effectivenesss of such methods is temporary. At judgment, one of the reasons a Christian will have confidence is because he has lived as Jesus lived (I John 4:17). The Diotrephes-people will be running for the rocks and hills. People who think they are "big" will become small when the King of kings returns. The church has only one head, and that head does not like others acting as if they were the heads.

B. *For a Person of God,* v. 12

> **Demetrius has received a good testimony from every one, and from the truth itself; and we also bear witness, and you know that our witness is true (v. 12).**

Why did John recommend Demetrius? We do not know for certain; however, the context suggests that Demetrius was probably one of those persons whom Diotrephes had refused hospitality. Perhaps Demetrius was expected to be in the area again soon. In fact, he might be delivering this letter to Gaius.

Who is Demetrius? We aren't sure, but a couple of possible candidates are interesting. One is the Demetrius from Ephesus who was a maker of idols (Acts 19). If so, then he had been converted. Since John spent his final years in Ephesus, this could be the same Demetrius. Wouldn't that drive Diotrephes up the wall — to provide room and board to a former manufacturer of idols?

Some suggest that Demetrius was the Demas who had deserted Paul and had since repented and returned to the church (Col. 4:14; II Tim. 4:10; Demas may be short for Demetrius). Materially supporting a former dropout would also upset the Diotrephes-mentality. If you doubt that, just watch what happens when a preacher who went astray morally or doctrinally later gives that up and tries to preach again. "Once a backslider, always a backslider" is the Diotrephes' response.

But over against stigmatizing Demetrius with false accusations are three commendations — (1) **from everyone,** (2) **from the truth itself** — evidently from the fruit of the truth being expressed from his life, (3) from John — **we also bear witness.**

IV. *A Resolution,* vv. 13, 14

I had many things to write to you, but I am not willing to write them to you with pen and ink; but I hope to see you shortly, and we shall speak face to face. Peace be to you. The friends greet you. Greet the friends by name (vv. 13, 14).

John planned to continue travelling and speaking (see note on II John 12, 13). What a way to live out a full life. He knew nothing about a mandatory retirement. Nor did he look forward to retirement by the beach or in the desert, but instead to responsibilities with the brethren.

While both II and III John end with a greeting from others, John added a significant note to III John, **peace be to you.** That was no doubt in contrast to what Diotrephes was offering. Diotrephes headed up a warfare, not a peace.

Christian peace is always to be expressed in two directions — upward to God (Rom. 5:1) and outward to others (Rom. 14:19). To eliminate one is to also erase the other. That's why the Gaius-mentality must be honored, while the Diotrephes-mentality must be rejected.

Gaius had not only been a friend (vv. 5-6), but he also had friends — **the friends greet you.** These may have been all the members of the church where John lived, or it might have been those individuals in John's presence who had been cared for by Gaius' hospitality.

What a beautiful way to describe the comradeship and fellowship of God's family — **friends.** That's what Diotrephes was not. But that's what we *all* need — Christian **friends.** And that's also what we all need to be to others — **friends** who care so much that we can greet one another **by name.** The nonpersonal gives way to the personal. Why? Because we're **friends.** Be one — and you'll have many. And as that happens — **peace** will **be to you.**

QUESTIONS FOR DISCUSSION:

1. How does a hospitable Christian spread joy?
2. Do we trust Christian strangers?
3. How do we show hospitality to Christian strangers today? Or how do we fail to do so?
4. List ways you, your class, and your congregation could improve in this area of life.
5. Do you or your church hesitate to support the preachers and missionaries connected with your congregation? Why or why not?
6. In what specific ways is the mentality of Diotrephes still alive today? What damage does it do?
7. Who has the right to act like Diotrephes today?
8. Why do the Diotrephes-type of people often have more influence in the church? What can be done about it?

A SELECTED BIBLIOGRAPHY
FOR THE PERSON IN THE PEW

BARCLAY, William. *The Letters of John and Jude,* rev. ed., Philadelphia: Westminster, 1976.

GILL, Clinton. *Hereby We Know.* Joplin, MO: College Press, 1966.

MARSHALL, I. Howard. *The Epistles of John.* Grand Rapids: Eerdmans, 1978.

McDOWELL, Edward. "1-2-3 John" in *The Broadman Commentary,* vol. 12. Nashville: Broadman, 1972.

MOODY, Dale. *The Letters of John.* Waco, TX: Word Books, 1970.

PLUMMER, Alfred. *The Epistles of S. John.* Cambridge: University Press, 1883.

ROBERTS, J. W. *The Letters of John.* Austin, TX: R. B. Sweet Co., 1968.

ROSS, Alexander. *The Epistles of James and John.* Grand Rapids: Eerdmans, 1954.

STOTT, John. *The Epistles of John.* Grand Rapids: Eerdmans, 1964.